Super Brain:
Strategies to Upgrade Your Brain, Unlock Your Potential, Perform at Your Peak, and Achieve Anything

By Peter Hollins,
Author and Researcher at petehollins.com

Table of Contents

CHAPTER 1. THE UNIVERSE INSIDE OUR HEADS 7

A BASIC INTRODUCTION TO YOUR BRAIN   9
NEUROPLASTICITY   19

CHAPTER 2. THE BRAIN IS NOT PERFECT, BUT WE CAN WORK WITH IT   41

CONNECTIONS AND HABITS ARE KEY; YOU CAN'T USE WHAT YOU DON'T HAVE   44
THE LIMITS OF OUR ATTENTION   57
FLAWS IN OUR THINKING: COGNITIVE BIASES   72
OUR IDENTITY IMPROVES OUR HABITS   81

CHAPTER 3. PEAK PERFORMANCE AND EXECUTIVE FUNCTIONING   91

FOLLOW THE RHYTHM   91
OUR BRAIN LIKES FUN AND EASY: WHY WE PROCRASTINATE   100
DISENGAGING YOUR BRAIN'S AUTOPILOT   110
INVESTING TIME INTO EXECUTIVE SKILLS   116
EMOTIONAL REGULATION   126
WORKING MEMORY   131

CHAPTER 4. HOW THE BRAIN LEARNS — 139

WEAVING A STRONG NEURAL NETWORK — 141
TWO THINKING MODES — 147
LESS INFORMATION IS MORE — 151
PAVLOV AND HIS DOGS — 155
MAKE LEARNING MORE FUN — 159
DEEP PROCESSING — 163

CHAPTER 5. HOW THE BRAIN MEMORIZES — 169

FORGETTING — 174
THE FORGETTING CURVE — 177
THE STUDY CYCLE — 180
RETRIEVAL PRACTICE — 185
SPACED REPETITION — 192

SUMMARY GUIDE — 203

Chapter 1. The Universe Inside Our Heads

One of the most amazing things that exist today is the brain. The brain is an elaborate structure made up of billions of individual neurons that form complicated networks. Though we've gained a considerable understanding of how other organs in the human body work, the brain is science's final frontier, and we are just now grasping the secrets of consciousness, intelligence, creativity and more. It's no exaggeration to say that our brains are what make us human, and are tremendously complex and capable of achieving almost anything we want.

We often take our brains for granted - after all, we live with them every day, with the good and the bad. However, even right this moment as your eyes scan this page, it is performing an impressive range of tasks, such as keeping your body alive and your lungs breathing to storing the entirety of your life experiences and allowing you to read this text as dozens of other "programs" are working in the background. Our brains allow us to learn and master languages, some of the most complex systems that not even the best supercomputers can handle with our efficiency. Human interactions that rely on verbal and non-verbal signals, and millions of bits of information that help us engage with the world around us are also being processed easily. Not too shabby.

But we can use our brains to do so much more and often let our potential just sit there untouched. Fortunately, just like the body muscles can be strengthened to their fullest potential, the brain can be supported to do what it does best. When we learn how it works, its habits and flaws, we can consciously use all the wonderful opportunities and resources it has to shape our lives in line with what we desire.

In the following chapters, we will talk about several evidence-based techniques that will help you take advantage of your brain's functioning to achieve the best results in your daily life. It's fair to say that your lived experience is fundamentally shaped by your brain – change your brain, and the whole world changes. In this book, we will be exploring specific practical techniques, and walking through them step by step, showing you how to make the best use of the miracle that is your human brain. But first, we will talk about the brain in general: what it is, how it works, and its unique characteristics.

A basic introduction to your brain

Structure

In biology, structure follows function, so let's look at the brain's structure to grasp its function. Your brain is the control center for every part of your body and everything you do, consciously and unconsciously. It directs all processes, from the most basic to the most complicated ones. The brain is part of the central nervous system, with your spinal cord. The nerves in the spinal cord send signals to the rest of the body and bring sensory information back to the control center

(Jawabri & Sharma, 2021, Physiology, Cerebral Cortex Functions).

The brain consists of three parts: the brain stem, the cerebellum, and the cerebral cortex. The brain stem takes care of the basic functions, like breathing, while the cerebellum is involved with movement and balance. However, the brain's cortex truly distinguishes us as a species (NBA, 2020, Brain Structure and Function). This so-called "higher" part of the brain was the last to evolve in our evolutionary history.

Other animals rely much more on the stem and the cerebellum than the cortex, and theirs is not nearly as elaborate as ours. One remarkable example of this is the case of Mike, a chicken that survived without its head for a good 18 months. The reason for this was that the chicken lost his head, the stem and the cerebellum, mostly, were left intact (Crew, 2014). This is a feat that no human could repeat.

While the more ancient parts of the brain are responsible for everything required for basic survival, the cortex is in charge of the most complex and higher order cognitive functions such as thinking, language, memory, logical, judgment, morality, and more. It comprises two hemispheres joined by the corpus callosum, which oversees communication between the two. It also comprises four lobes: frontal, parietal, temporal, and occipital. The frontal lobe is mostly associated with decision-making, reasoning, morality, and similar functions (Jawabri & Sharma, 2021, Physiology, Cerebral Cortex Functions).

There are some key structures in the brain with important and specific functions, although it's important to remember that most parts of the brain have multiple duties and can compensate for each other if there is damage to any one zone. Because most complex cognitive functions require many skills, we can think of the brain as working holistically, with many areas activating in concert with one another. We will mention two structures that are especially important and will help us in later chapters.

The amygdala is part of the limbic system, a brain circuit that deals with emotions, reactions, and their processing. Its main function involves reacting to dangerous situations and stimulating the fight or flight response processed in other structures, like the brain stem (Pessoa, 2010, Emotion and Cognition and the Amygdala: From "what is it?" to "what's to be done?").

The amygdala also is connected to memory formation. Memories of traumatic events are processed by the amygdala and stored with vivid detail, as are events seen as dangerous. This structure is connected to experiences of fear and anxiety, but also seems tied to the processing and formations of positive and negative memories with emotional elements (Pessoa, 2010, Emotion and Cognition and the Amygdala: From "what is it?" to "what's to be done?").

The memories tied to emotions seem stronger and more important for our brain than those that involve no emotion. This will be important to remember when we discuss how to improve your memory, but knowing how the brain processes emotions gives us valuable clues about mastering emotional self-regulation, improving motivation, and combatting addiction and trauma.

The hippocampus is the structure that works to consolidate memories and move them to our long-term memory - the storage that keeps what we learn throughout our lives. It is also connected with visuo-spatial orientation or how well we can navigate the world. However, its central role is helping us make lasting memories, as people with a damaged hippocampus lose that ability and experience something known as anterograde amnesia: they cannot make new memories (Allen, 2018, Classic and recent advances in understanding amnesia). Naturally, if you're interested in improving your brain's ability to learn, you'll want to understand the hippocampus so that you can work with it rather than against it.

Neurons and neurotransmitters

The brain is not merely a collection of separate modules, each responsible for a different function. Instead, its characteristics stem from the fact that it's a *network* between these many nodes, and what matters is the degree and nature of connectivity between the neural cells. We have around 86 billion neurons. For comparison, there are around 200 billion stars in the Milky Way. Our brain is not quite a galaxy, but it comprises at least half of one. Other animals have significantly fewer neurons than we do: a regular monkey might have around a billion, for instance, although other primates have more. An elephant has around 6 billion neurons, and even the killer whale, with its massive brain, has only around 43 billion (Herculano-Houzel, 2019, Longevity and sexual maturity vary across species with number of cortical neurons, and humans are no exception).

Each neuron is a cell, and it mainly passes on information to other neurons. A neuron has two types of "tentacles" protruding from its body: dendrites and an axon. The dendrites of each neuron will reach out to other cells' axons but never quite touch them. Instead, they will make a connection by sending electric signals and releasing chemicals called neurotransmitters that get released into the microscopic space between the cells called synapses (Hawkins & Ahmad, 2016, Why Neurons Have Thousands of Synapses, a Theory of Sequence Memory in Neocortex).

Neurons talk to each other electrochemically across the spaces between the dendrites and axons of the cells. When there is an electric signal, a neurotransmitter is released into the gap and attaches itself to the other neuron through its receptors. When two neurons fire together, they become connected. One neuron can have between one and 100,000 synapses. That is, it can be connected to as many as 100,000 other neurons. On average, a neuron has 1000 synapses (Nguyen, 2010, Total Number of Synapses in the Adult Human Neocortex). Imagine all those 86 billion neurons, each with around 1000 connections – impressive!

The neurons can send different messages to each other through brain chemicals called neurotransmitters. A neurotransmitter can pass on three types of messages to get the other neuron to do something or prevent it from doing something, to stimulate or inhibit, and thus complex messages and information are encoded and transmitted rapidly throughout the brain. There are over100 different neurotransmitters (Sheffer, Reddi, & Phillarisetty, 2021, Physiology,

Neurotransmitters), but the most important ones are:

- Dopamine

Dopamine is a hormone and also a neurotransmitter associated with the anticipation of rewards. It is involved in motivation, with wanting more and the satisfaction of getting a surprise or receiving a reward. When we feel disappointed, our dopamine dives. It is also linked to alertness and motor control (Ubuka, 2021, Handbook of hormones).

- Serotonin

Serotonin is a hormone and neurotransmitter tied to mood regulation, so it's involved in problems like anxiety and depression. It also helps regulate sleep, appetite, and learning. It can be found in the gut and the brain and is linked to digestion (Bancos, 2018, What is Serotonin?).

- Oxytocin

Oxytocin is associated with bonding and love. It is tied with physical contact with others and prosocial and altruistic behavior, and the creation of social memories and aggression. Oxytocin modulates the expression of aggressive and bonding behaviors (Roopaspree, Jophy, & Mukkadan, 2019, Oxytocin-functions: an overview).

- Norepinephrine

Norepinephrine is a hormone and neurotransmitter that increases attention and is associated with the brain's stress response. It also increases heart rate and blood pressure, as well as sugar levels to give a boost of energy to the body (Donnell et al., 2012, Norepinephrine: A Neuromodulator That Boosts the Function of Multiple Cell Types to Optimize CNS Performance).

- Endorphins

Endorphins are associated with pain relief and produce a sense of reward. They reduce discomfort and also are involved with rewarding behaviors. That is, they promote the experience of pleasure in different situations, like when you laugh (Chaudry & Gossman, 2021, Biochemistry, Endorphin).

Besides this, it's worth mentioning cortisol. Cortisol is not a neurotransmitter but regulates how these get released. It is a hormone related to stress and has positive and negative effects. It helps us stay more alert, but too much cortisol wears the body down and leads to health problems (Thau, Gandhi, & Sharma, 2021, Physiology, Cortisol).

Neurotransmitters play different functions, and we can influence their release, as well as the release of various hormones through our habits. This brings us to another important and unexpected part of the "brain" – the gut and its microbiome.

The brain in the gut: the enteric nervous system

In addition to our central nervous system, there is the enteric nervous system, a relatively recent discovery. It refers to the 100 million neurons that line our gastrointestinal tract throughout its length, called the ENS or the brain-gut axis (Carabotti, 2015, The gut-brain axis: interactions between enteric microbiota, central and enteric nervous systems).

Our gut also has nerve cells, and it is connected to the central nervous system, particularly the brain, through the vagus nerve. The gut also requires neurotransmitters to function and make new neurons when required. The bacteria in the gut also plays an important role in the functioning of the ENS because it produces certain neurochemicals (Rao & Gershon, 2016, The bowel and beyond: the enteric nervous system in neurological disorders).

The ENS can act independently from the brain to regulate gastrointestinal functions without intervention from the brain, but they are connected in many other ways. Problems with the brain can also manifest in the gut, and it also shows one way our brain and our body are linked (Rao & Gershon, 2016, The bowel and beyond: the enteric nervous system in neurological disorders). Digestive issues can appear because of problems with our mental health, while improving the gut biome can positively affect our overall well-being.

Neuroplasticity

Our brain is complex (remember, it has about as many neurons as stars in half a galaxy), and we are only beginning to understand how it operates. Most of our knowledge was developed in the 20th and 21st centuries, and most of that came from the past few decades, so still much a work in progress. And still, there is a lot we now know and understand.

We know that our brains work through complex networks and connections, and that all the information inside our heads is organized through association.

One of the most amazing discoveries we have made about the brain is understanding its neuroplasticity. For a long time, it was believed that the brain was shaped in a particular way and developed only until adolescence. It was also believed that we had a few neurons and, throughout our adult lives, could only use neurons and neuronal connections already formed. Thankfully, this was proven wrong (Kwik, 2020, Limitless: Upgrade Your Brain, Learn Anything Faster, and Unlock Your Exceptional Life). Our brains continue to produce new neurons throughout life through a process known as neurogenesis, making new connections, and getting rid of old connections that are no longer useful. It's true that kids have the most plastic brains out there, but adults do not lose this characteristic.

Our brains develop throughout our lives. They are blessed with neuroplasticity: the ability to be shaped and molded by our behaviors, environment, and habits. This is a different model of the brain – rather than seeing it as a fixed organ that does just one predetermined job; it is instead an organ that is in dynamic *relationship* with the environment, and can grow, respond, adapt and change depending on the environmental demands.

Neuroplasticity means that whatever we do can change how our brains operate and more than that, how they are wired throughout our lives. It means we can use our brains to work on our brains; we can tweak our environment to adjust our brains – by using our brains! This means that even if we faced adverse factors such as poverty throughout our childhood, which impacted our brain, it could be rewired by a different set of circumstances and different choices.

Eleanor Maguire did the classic study you will always see mentioned when talking about neuroplasticity. She focused on cab drivers who had to prepare to earn their licenses by memorizing specific parts of the city with thousands of streets, corners, attractions, and turns. It takes around four years to complete the practice, and only about 50% pass the licensing test. Maguire expected those who did, that lucky half, might have had a bigger hippocampus - the brain's structure tied to memory (Maguire et al., 2000, Navigation-related structural change in the hippocampi of taxi drivers).

What Maguire found instead is that the cab drivers, because of their experience and study, as well as their years driving around London, enhanced their hippocampus. This structure became bigger and more full of connections because of the work the drivers had done to memorize routes and streets (Maguire et al., 2000, Navigation-related structural change in the hippocampi of taxi drivers).

A study focusing on a boy who lost nearly one-third of his brain due to an unavoidable surgery discovered that after this procedure, the boy retained his previous abilities and even improved on some measures of IQ (Liu et al., 2013, Successful Reorganization of Category-Selective Visual Cortex following Occipito-temporal Lobectomy in Childhood). Even though this does not happen in every similar case, other areas of his brain took on the functions of those that got removed. His brain was adaptable enough to deal with something as serious as losing big chunks of the visual processing centers. Neuroplasticity can help people recover from serious injuries to the brain, but it can also modify how we live our daily lives.

Neuroplasticity is associated with physical changes in the brain, like those that happened with the cab drivers who made their hippocampi bigger. It also involves changes in neuronal networks, for example, through the connections the cells make with each other, the generation of new neurons, and neurobiochemical changes, for example, the release of more or less dopamine and serotonin (Fuchs & Flugge, 2014, Adult Neuroplasticity: More Than 40 Years of Research). All this constantly changes throughout our lives.

In a disorder like depression, there is a dysfunctional release of serotonin. There is a low level of the chemical, which leads to a low mood and problems with appetite and sleep. A certain relationship is set up with the brain and the environment – the brain takes shape to function in a way characteristic of depression. However, medication can increase serotonin levels and change the brain from within, while therapy and lifestyle changes work on the surrounding environment to change the brain from the outside (Cowen & Browning, 2015, What has serotonin to do with depression?).

This means that our choices every day shape our brain to be and function differently. Something as simple as learning a new bit of information can mean a new connection between two neurons not connected before while repeating that bit of information means making that connection sturdier.

Our brain can amaze things thanks to neuroplasticity. Your abilities and skills are not set in stone, nor is your neurobiology.

Understanding the brain

So, your brain is amazing and capable of achieving plenty of fascinating tasks. After seeing them once, people can memorize hundreds of numbers without being blessed with a prodigious memory. We can learn any skill if we decide to do it. Our limits are often self-imposed and not objective. At the same time, there are better and more effective ways to learn and boost our brains. What holds us back is our belief that we can't do something and a lack of knowledge that makes us pick ineffective strategies.

We need to consider how our brain works. For example, if we learn a new language by memorizing separate words, we might learn a few phrases, but we will not master this new skill. Trying to memorize a language by remembering separate words means we do not understand how our brains work and how language settles into our neural networks.

Each cognitive process we have, such as learning, memory, habit formation, emotional regulation, and self-control, among many others, are tied to how our brain functions. Once we understand this, we can choose better strategies to change any habit and any aspect of our life causing us trouble. While there are objective limits, they are often very different and much less severe than we might imagine.

Here is a question. If you had to prepare for a test next week, evaluating your understanding of a text, which strategy would you choose? Many people would repeatedly reread the text, underlining the most important parts and points. But these strategies have been proven ineffective! We know that our brain doesn't respond well to them (Biwer et al., 2020, Fostering Effective Learning Strategies in Higher Education – A Mixed-Methods Study).

Understanding how our brains work can help us choose efficient strategies, get better results that are more lasting and less difficult to achieve because we use means that align with our neural wiring.

We can reach great results thanks to consistent work to strengthen neuronal networks. We now know that strengthening one connection can weaken others – a perfect explanation for why we need new habits to replace older ones (Jenks et al., 2021 Heterosynaptic Plasticity and the Experience-

Dependent Refinement of Developing Neuronal Circuits).

We can change our brains and change our lives. We just need to know how.

What can affect our neuroplasticity?

In these sections, we will do a deep and practical dive into how you can better understand your brain and use specific, focused techniques to improve different aspects of your life and use the flaws in your brain's processing to make your day-to-day easier and more satisfying. Fortunately, the brain is neuroplastic – but it is not endlessly so, and we need to know the rules for how it organizes itself to take advantage of its adaptability.

Before getting to specific techniques, we will talk a little about the general ways to keep our brains happy and healthy and ready to enhance their neuroplastic capacity, because it's not always the same. Some things and factors can reduce our brain's capacity to adapt.

Let's start with a few general things all brain owners need to remember to have them prepared to adapt and shift.

- **Physical activity**

Physical activity can lead to greater neuroplasticity. Exercise not only counteracts cognitive decline but can also encourage our brains to start producing new neurons and improve our ability to make and change connections. Daily physical activities, like chores or walking, and focused exercise are linked to benefits for cerebrovascular health and a higher ability to learn and memorize (Mandolesi et al., 2017, Environmental Factors Promoting Neural Plasticity: Insights from Animal and Human Studies).

- **Sleep**

Getting enough sleep is an essential condition for neuroplasticity. It promotes repair, memory consolidation, and restorative processes across all animal life. Chronic sleep deprivation disrupts neuroplasticity because it can also negatively affect learning and memory. Recent research suggests that we need uninterrupted sleep to effectively make lasting neural connections because memories get consolidated in stages. Breaking up our sleep time or not getting to REM or deep sleep means that some forms of memories and connections are never made fully or never consolidated. Besides this, sleep can restore plasticity for the next day (Mandolesi et al., 2017, Environmental Factors Promoting Neural Plasticity: Insights from Animal and Human Studies).

- **Diet and nutrition**

Our brain consumes over 20% of the energy we derive from nutrients. Nutrients are needed for neuroplasticity, and eating patterns help or hinder changes in brain structure.

We can say, for instance, that too much sugar in the absence of healthy fats, can make learning and memory much less effective, and specific substances in foods make our brains more malleable and help create stronger connections.

The first ingredient is polyphenol, found in fruit, vegetables, tea, juices, plants, and some herbs. They can reduce the effects of cognitive decline and stress while improving synaptic plasticity. Polyphenols can be found in curcumin and omega-3 fatty acids that appear to be essential for good plasticity (Murphy, Dias, & Thuret, 2014, Effects of diet on brain plasticity in animal and human studies: mind the gap).

Evidence shows that eating curcumin and drinking teas, especially green tea, black tea, and oolong tea, helps neuroplasticity. Other types of food associated with improvements in cognitive functioning are grapes, wine, and peanuts, thanks to their content of resveratrol. Omega-3 fatty acids, found in oily fish like salmon and anchovies, also are linked to improved plasticity (Wang, Li, Xu, Song, Tao, & Bai Y, 2012 Green tea epigallocatechin-3-gallate (EGCG) promotes neural progenitor cell proliferation and sonic hedgehog pathway activation during adult hippocampal neurogenesis; Conklin, et al., 2007 Long-chain omega-3 fatty acid intake is associated positively with corticolimbic gray matter volume in healthy adults; Cox, Pipingas, Scholey, 2015, Investigation of the effects of solid lipid curcumin on cognition and mood in a healthy older population).

So, the foods and supplements that can help your brain become even more malleable include:

- Curcumin
- Green tea
- Black tea
- Oolong tea
- Grapes
- Wine
- Grape juice
- Fatty fishes, like salmon, herring, anchovies, etc.
- Omega-3 supplements

- Peanuts

Adding more foods that promote neuroplasticity to your diet can help make changes more successful and lasting. Give your brain the food it craves and feed it like a champion.

- **Consistency**

Traumatic events can leave a lasting impact on the brain, even if they only happen once. However, to change our neural connections, we need to be consistent and build on them every day or almost every day.

Making habits is not just a behavioral change: it leads to long-lasting changes in the dorsolateral striatum or DLS, and this is a separate part of the brain from the one that regulates goal-driven behavior. When habits become automatic, they save a lot of energy, and our brain turns to them first, so healthier habits allow us to rewire specific structures to change our automatic patterns of responses and behaviors (Malvaez, 2020, Neural substrates of habit). Consistency allows us to engage the dorsolateral striatum rather than other parts of our brain. One important suggestion here is to put things into practice every day, even if it is just for a few minutes. If you must skip, try to skip a single time and not twice in a row, as that can disrupt your habits and cost you a significant chunk of your progress.

A good example of the importance of persistence is the situation of stroke survivors, many of whom recover brain functioning. One of the key elements for recovering and developing neuroplasticity is for people to repeat the same tasks repeatedly (Hatem, Saussez, Della Faille, Prist, Zhang, Dispa, & Bleyenheuft, 2016, Rehabilitation of Motor Function after Stroke: A Multiple Systematic Review Focused on Techniques to Stimulate Upper Extremity Recovery).

Reluctance and resistance

Not everything about the brain is positive. Sometimes, its functioning is associated with issues, particularly as the brain tends to have processing errors. We will discuss them more in-depth in the following chapters, but it's important to note that even though our brains are made for malleability, they tend to resist change.

Established patterns tend to win due to the effects of the dorsolateral striatum that can override our desire to reach specific goals (Malvaez, 2020, Neural substrates of habit). It's not a sign that something is going wrong, and we should expect lapses, especially when tired and stressed. Remember that your brain likes saving energy and is conservative in this sense, preferring established behavior patterns until they change enough to become the new routine.

Stress

Chronic and intense stress can negatively impact our neuroplasticity, rewiring our brain to be more vulnerable to new stressors. It can contribute to depression and anxiety by changing the functioning of our neural networks (Singh & Karkare, 2017, Stress, Depression and Neuroplasticity). It's important to reduce stress to focus the effects of our neuroplasticity on positive aspects and make changes for the better.

Continued stress can make parts of our neurons atrophy: they start growing slowly and are less able to make successful connections, which leads to a worse memory and learning ability. Fewer neurons are produced, and synapses get disrupted (Singh & Karkare, 2017, Stress, Depression and Neuroplasticity). Stress is a factor that can negatively impact our neuroplasticity.

Our brain is a wonderful structure, and we are only getting to know how it operates. We have different empirically proven strategies that can help us modify our neural networks to achieve our desired results. But, our brain is not perfect. It often does things we wish it wouldn't do and is prone to errors in very particular patterns. It has real limitations. By acknowledging this, we can reach better results. The next chapter will consider patterns of functioning that the brain shows and how this can be applied to specific techniques for achieving beneficial goals.

What's the point?

Cool, so we know now a little more about our brains. But what's the point of that? First, this section helps us lay the groundwork for the techniques we will be discussing later on. It introduced the most important concepts and the basic principles under which the brain works. We will clarify how each technique connects to your brain's functioning in these sections, but the goal is also to understand *why* each technique works and evaluate its effects on the brain. Knowing this can help these strategies feel more grounded.

The second goal of this brief introduction is to provide more information about how your brain operates. We all have brains, but we often remain woefully misinformed about how they function. This can empower us to make better choices when we can consider our control center with its limitations and preferences. We don't get to change everything about our brain and must take it into account.

The third reason is to help you reconsider some of your limiting beliefs. We often feel we have reached our limits or that some skills are beyond us. We might believe that it is too late to do new things or acquire new habits. But once you consider the neuroscience behind it all, it becomes evident that you can. Our brains, by their design, can inspire things and hold within them a huge potential.

So, let's look at the more practical side of things. Now that we know the basic elements of how our brain operates, let's examine evidence-based techniques based on neuroscience for better results in learning, changing your habits, reaching your full potential, and more.

Takeaways

- The brain is a truly amazing organ and it lies at the very heart of what makes us human beings. To maximize our own potential, we need to learn how our brains work, why, and what we can do to support our innate capacities for maximum wellbeing.
- The brain's structure tells us a lot about its function. It forms part of the body's overall central nervous system. There are three main parts: the brain stem, the cerebellum, and the "higher brain" or cerebral cortex,

further divided into four sections. The brain is made of billions of neurons connected neurochemically across gaps called synapses.
- The gut and its microbiome are like a "second brain" and the gut and brain are intimately connected.
- The amygdala is important for emotional processing, and the hippocampus is heavily involved in memory. Key neurotransmitters include serotonin and dopamine, although there are over 100 neurotransmitters in the brain.
- Many brain disorders and mental health issues are understood to correlate with certain chemical brain states, and the brain also possesses flaws and weaknesses that make it prone to malfunctioning.
- Neuroplasticity is the brain's ability to change and adapt to reflect demands from the environment. This means that neural connections can be "rewired," and the brain can evolve, adapt, and change, not just in childhood but throughout life.
- Many things affect neuroplasticity, such as stress, physical activity, sleep, illness, diet and other lifestyle factors. If we

understand how to work with our brain's innate capacity to change itself, we can use specially designed techniques to maximize on our potential.

Chapter 2. The Brain Is Not Perfect, But We Can Work With It

We have said many positive things about the brain and its amazing capabilities. While they are deserved, and neuroplasticity suggests that our brains are infinitely adaptable and malleable, this raises the question of why we struggle so much with our goals, habits, and practices. You're probably reading this book precisely because you wish your brain performed better in one way or another! If our brains are so well-evolved to deal with life, why do we struggle so much with them?

There are two key aspects to the answer. First, clearly, we don't always know how to use our inbuilt brain mental capacities or how to apply the best strategies. Think about it – *how* to use your brain (versus just the content you put into it!) is something we rarely get taught in school or anywhere else, even though knowing how to learn or change our habits could give us a major boost in literally every aspect of our lives (Kwik, 2020, Limitless: Upgrade Your Brain, Learn Anything Faster, and Unlock Your Exceptional Life). So, it's a question of lack of knowledge and understanding.

The second reason is that our brain is not perfect. It *is* amazing, but it is also a flawed and complicated organ, just like any other. It functions in particular ways with real limitations we need to acknowledge. Remember, it's a physical organ and *not a computer*! It would be foolish to deny these basic flaws or principles, but we can get the best results quickly when we acknowledge our natural limitations and work intelligently around them.

In the next chapters, we will explore various techniques to help you achieve your goals. Each is based on the brain's biochemistry and its function, and supported by scientific evidence. However, the techniques are general and should be adapted to your particular situation and objectives.

The goal is to provide strategies based on the principles upon which the brain naturally operates. You can use these techniques to achieve your goals, as they are general and help you enhance your skill development, personal and professional growth, time management, and learning – or whatever else you'd like your brain to create for you! With this much possibility, it's good to see concrete examples in action, though, so each technique will also come with specific examples. Then it's your job to see how the technique can be applied to your own life, and whatever is especially relevant for you now.

Each technique comes with a short introduction explaining the theory behind it to give a broader context and all the details for the technique. Each is meant to be generalizable to different areas of your life.

We will first consider the tips we can find by recognizing the limitations our brain naturally has to turn them to your advantage and reduce the negative impact these limitations might have on your life. The techniques have a broad purpose and apply to any goals you want to reach, such as exercising regularly, living a healthier life, acquiring a new profession, or building a stronger relationship with yourself.

After this, we will focus on learning and all the best strategies for learning any skills or knowledge you want in your life. The techniques offer a way to learn that sticks with you and offers long-term results faster and with greater returns.

Connections and habits are key; you can't use what you don't have

We can't use what isn't there. Simple, right? Unless you have the proper connections and these are strong enough, you will struggle with different tasks and skills. The things we want to do well need to be practiced more than those we don't care about, and we can't expect to perform well in anything we have not practiced before. The brain cannot instantly pick up new skills, and it requires practice before a habit settles down. So, if you've ever tried to pick up a new habit – and failed – you'll know why. It takes a lot more time than you might think!

This applies not only to specific skills, like speaking a new language, playing a musical instrument, or drawing. It also applies to more general abilities and functions that underlie a variety of situations and can have a huge effect on our daily lives. For example, self-control can improve with practice, as can emotional regulation, attention, memory, etc. By focusing on these underlying cognitive processes, we can earn massive gains across many areas of our lives.

Neuroplasticity can help improve many things, even those we might consider intrinsic to ourselves or just something that has always been a particular way. If you have never been able to do this or that, neuroplasticity can mold that in many cases. But again, it takes time. You are not just abstractly changing your mind – you are literally and physiologically changing the connections between neurons and altering the structure of the tissues in your brain. So be patient!

For example, it is clear that ADHD or attention deficit disorder is a neurological condition that affects many areas of a person's life and has a basis in the way the brain is structured and functions. This condition is chronic, but with brain training, individuals with ADHD can improve their ability to pay attention and restructure their brains. While it is not a full solution to ADHD, it shows there is always room for improvement with neuroplasticity (Mishra, Mizrenich & Sagar, 2013, Accessible online neuroplasticity-targeted training for children with ADHD).

Technique #1 Automation and trigger-routine-reward

So, we know that neuroplasticity can help us make new connections that lead to new habits becoming stronger with practice. "Neurons that wire together, fire together" basically means that every time you use a certain neural pathway, you cement it, and make it more likely to fire again next time. We also know that our brains work through associations with the connections we build on a neural level. Using these two key principles of neural functioning, we will learn to automate our habits through the habit loop.

How it all connects to the brain: We create habits through neuroplasticity and the neural networks that are the building blocks of our brain's architecture. But the brain relies on habits representing the strongest connections between neurons to get us through the day. Habits are also a primary influence on our brain's functioning and structure because they get repeated and reinforced over and over.

Habits are what shape our brains, no doubt about it. We repeat actions so much that they form strong synaptic connections – literal shortcuts in the brain. This is a good thing since it means your brain can free up energy if it does things on autopilot. But not all habits are beneficial, obviously. Repeated actions have small but cumulative effects, so the best way to make a change is to shift into habits to serve us better. This is not quantum leap territory, but rather a slow-and-steady rewiring.

Without habits, our brain would become overwhelmed, and constructing the right framework can help us save energy for what truly matters. If people lose the ability to make habits due to brain damage, they become unable to focus on anything and perform basic activities, so caught up in uncertainty, they cannot function (Duhigg, 2014, The Power of Habit: Why We Do What We Do in Life and Business). Being automatic isn't necessarily a problem – but you want to make the *right* things automatic. Habits determine our levels of happiness and success much more than other factors, simply because of this cumulative effect and because they enable us to reach the best results.

Author James Clear has popularized the habit loop, but we can find similar ideas in research too. The loop involves various elements we need to construct to create a new habit successfully (Clear, Atomic Habits; Gardener, 2012, Making health habitual: the psychology of 'habit-formation' and general practice).

- **Trigger/cue**

The trigger or cue is the first step. It is an internal or external experience that will signal that it's time for the habit. Here are a few examples.

You feel hungry (cue = hunger), so you eat. You pick up your phone and check your messages (cue = boredom). Your alarm rings, and you get up to hit snooze (cue = the alarm). This is the start of the loop.

- **Response/routine**

This is the habit per se. What will you do when you experience the cue? Some people smoke when stressed or grab a snack whenever they walk by the kitchen. Others exercise after waking up. The routine or response you have to the cue is the behavior you might want to show in the circumstances. The response and the cue don't necessarily have to relate to one another, and the routine can be beneficial or harmful.

- **Reward**

The reward is the experience you get at the end. It might be the sweet taste of a treat or seeing a new email or new message you wanted to get. A habit can become cemented even if you don't get the reward every time.

Many habits, like checking our emails, become strong *because* they don't lead to the reward every time, only sometimes, and we never know when this reward will appear. This is called "intermittent reward" and it's what keeps gamblers hooked – the possibility there could be a reward just around the corner, so you'd better do the behavior once more just to see. Rewards reinforce behavior, and consolidate certain neural pathways. They're mediated by the brain's reward system and neurochemicals like dopamine.

Many of our habits are already streamlined, so we need not think about them. For example, you might have a strong loop of brushing your teeth: after eating, you brush them and experience the feeling of freshness. Once a habit is in place, you experience little or no effort to keep it running. Our healthy and unhealthy habits can operate with the same levels of automation too, so changing them is not about eradicating bad habits but replacing the ones you already have, creating new habits and breaking the existing loops.

We can kill two birds with one stone, replace some of the existing negative habits with healthier ones, and practice them until they become automatic. How long does it take for a habit to become a habit, that is, when your DLS takes over? You might have seen the 21 days figure, which gets repeated a lot, but this has been debunked. 21 days is a good first benchmark, but likely it will take more time than that (Welden et al., 2020, How to Form Good Habits? A Longitudinal Field Study on the Role of Self-Control in Habit Formation).

The second benchmark is 66 days. After 66 days, many people will already experience a habit as an automatic practice. However, it will still be important that you do it every day to avoid losing any gains (Lally, van Jaarsveld, Potts & Wardle, 2010, Modelling habit formation in the real world).

The third benchmark is 90 days. Over this time, you are certain to establish an automatic habit. Research suggests that it takes on average between 60 and 90 days to form a solid automated practice, so these are good goals to set for yourself to have more manageable timelines (Welden et al., 2020, How to Form Good Habits? A Longitudinal Field Study on the Role of Self-Control in Habit

Formation). Keeping a habit becomes easier each day, so you are unlikely to invest the same amounts of effort as time goes on, i.e., your effort will taper off. Consistency will ensure that it is easier each time to carry out the new habit.

The exact time frame likely depends on a mix of personality, circumstance and what you're trying to make a habit. Whatever the number, though, you can take advantage of the habit loop to create a new habit that helps you and doesn't hinder you. How? Easy: break down the habit into the three key parts: cue, response, and reward. Then reverse engineer it to use your inbuilt habit machinery to do the behavior you *choose*.

What is the cue that will signal that it's time for the behavior? Attach it to an existing situation that happens often and that you can't miss - waking up, hearing an alarm, getting a notification, the clock showing a specific time, etc. Find a consistent cue. To get rid of a bad habit, identify the cues that trigger that and attach a new response to this trigger.

Define the cue as clearly as you can and decide on your response. Keep it simple and manageable. You need to have a realistic response. If you have never gone running before, for example, don't set a goal of running for an hour every day at seven. Decide on ten minutes to start with. If you never get up early, don't expect you will be able to sustain a 6 am waking time all of a sudden. Unrealistic goals can be difficult to accomplish, and you are likely to drop the new habits before they form, which can make you feel disappointed and guilty. A consistently difficult habit might not be the best choice: think if there are similar responses you can use instead that are easier or if there is a way to make this response simpler for you (Kwik, 2020, Limitless: Upgrade Your Brain, Learn Anything Faster, and Unlock Your Exceptional Life). A small habit can have a big influence if you can be consistent about it.

Once you have established the response, consider the reward. Many bad habits have a clear reward. Smoking brings relaxation, and candy feels nice and gives us a little boost of dopamine plus energy associated with carbs. Good habits can sometimes be challenging because the reward is less obvious or immediate.

Because of this aspect, it's important to focus on your motivation. Why do you want this habit in your life? The more motivated you are, the easier it is to maintain a habit and create a reward. When you engage in the habit, focus on your satisfaction because you are achieving your goals. Find where the reward is in the new response: a pleasant sensation, the satisfaction of a job well-done, or any other experience that can help repeat the habit once again.

This creates two strong associations between the behavior, cue, and reward. First, your brain learns to engage in the behavior when the cue occurs and, second, has positive associations with the response. The habit becomes integrated into our brain's networks, and the associations grow stronger, so it gets easier each time to engage in the habit rather than in another behavior.

Having an established routine can help you save a lot of energy regarding automation. A routine does not require conscious effort or thought, which helps the brain reduce the energy it spends on these practices and makes it a lot easier to continue doing the things that work best for us. A routine that supports our goals is the best way to become healthier and improve our skills.

Gladwell (2008, Outliers) suggests that the key element for improving skill is practice, and practice is better when we do it consistently and mindfully. One of the best ways to practice the skills we want to develop is to create a routine that supports taking the time and effort to work on the skill every day or as often as possible. Automation means you need not make a conscious effort to engage in the practice but that your brain is consistently rewired to improve and grow your skills. 15 minutes every day is better than an hour once a week, and routines can help with this.

A routine is a series of habits that occur together. You will have at least a few habits that make up a routine, and some probably work well for you. The main aspect of changing a routine is targeting bad habits and working out new associations that help each habit connect with the other.

The keys to automation involve various elements. First, you can pre- make your decisions. What does this mean? You will decide on the routine and then carry it out time and time again, without making choices every day. While famously this is the kind of thing moguls like Steve Jobs and Mark Zuckerberg do with their clothes, for instance, it is an easy way to save your brain the effort and energy for daily choices. You can pre-make choices related to clothes, meal planning, organization, and, significantly, integrate everyday skill development without having to think about it. You don't have to make the choice to practice, you just do it, which helps your brain process it through a different structure and do it easier, faster, and more efficiently.

Here is an example. Anthony Trollope, the famously productive novelist, had the custom of writing for 15 minutes per hour, for three hours. He required himself to produce 250 words for each quarter. This allowed him to produce three novels of three volumes in the year when kept up consistently. This also illustrates the benefits of setting small goals and shows that simply making a manageable and effective habit can lead to huge gains over time (Clear, 2020, The 15-Minute Routine Anthony Trollope Used to Write 40+ Books).

The benefits of this are that you only have to choose once. You don't have to do all the internal process of convincing yourself to do it, of deciding what to do, etc. Our brain likes to save energy for better things too. Besides this, you can rewire your brain more consistently through small tasks repeated over and over again, much more so than through one-time events. Finally, it leads to great returns over time. You can find yourself achieving more through habits than other solutions.

We can do better when we focus on a single habit at a time. This is also based on a particular characteristic of our brain. Specifically, we can only pay attention to one thing at a time.

The limits of our attention

Attention is an important tool. It determines what we are focused on, and our attention can be directed voluntarily or involuntarily. At every moment, we are exposed to an endless stream of stimuli received by all our senses. We are also thinking, sensing, and experiencing a wide variety of internal things that also fight for our attention. Naturally, we have to filter the noise out to get to the point.

Our attention is optimized for this, and we can recognize that we do our best when we only pay attention to one thing. The state of flow, characterized by being immersed in a specific activity or task, is the one that leads to most productivity and allows us to be at our most creative (Grant, 2019, Productivity Isn't About Time Management. It's About Attention Management). In other terms, when we are only focused on one thing, our brains are operating at their best.

We have a limited attention capacity. We can think of it as a spotlight - we can only direct it at one thing at a time to become involved with this problem or task. There is debate as to whether we can only pay attention to one thing at a time or two or a few more (Gilchrist

& Cowan, 2011, Can the Focus of Attention Accommodate Multiple, Separate Items?). Still, strong evidence suggests that when we have to constantly switch between tasks, our cognitive capacity becomes lower (Madore & Wagner, 2020, Multicosts of Multitasking). We are not as able to do our best, and there are productivity costs that can become significant. A modern work or leisure environment is associated with an endless stream of distractions coming from social media, our phones, and generally from the demands that life places on our brains. When our environments are full of distraction, we are not operating at our best.

Some authors suggest that our brain does not have the architecture to perform two or more tasks simultaneously. While we can breathe, walk, and listen to music, our conscious attention and any tasks requiring it are more limited. We need not focus consciously to breathe and walk, so our brain may do other tasks. But if we are trying to have a conversation while writing a text, for example, or driving while talking on the phone, that's another matter.

As seen in neuroimaging studies, the brain struggles to process and complete two conscious tasks at once. This happens because our dorsal and ventral attention systems interact with the frontoparietal network. When we want to do a task, the frontoparietal network from our frontal lobe represents the goal that guides how we place attention. The dorsal network selects the information relevant to that task from our thoughts and the sensory information coming through (Madore & Wagner, 2020, Multicosts of Multitasking). One part of the brain outlines the goal and, using this goal. Other systems retrieve everything we need to accomplish it.

When we have more than one task, additional demands on the attention networks with limited capabilities. The ventral attention network, meanwhile, is focused on filtering out distracting information. When there is more when one task, this network also fails because there is information relevant to one task and irrelevant to the other, which interferes and makes people more likely to become distracted. All three networks need to work well to become fully focused on a task, and multitasking splits our attention and mixes up relevant and irrelevant information (Madore & Wagner, 2020, Multicosts of Multitasking).

Multitasking results in task switch costs. It's not that we can't try to multitask, it becomes more difficult, takes longer, and leads to worse outcomes. A switch cost involves reductions in accuracy, overall performance, or speed. It's unavoidable to have these costs when we have to switch between tasks because we are demanding more from the brain, and it's not optimized for that (Madore & Wagner, 2020, Multicosts of Multitasking).

We can't always avoid multitasking. In some jobs, it's especially prevalent and even expected. However, when working on our projects or organizing our tasks, we can do what we can to minimize switch costs and maximize our attention to help our brain operate with maximum capacity.

Technique #2: Attention management

As we have established that we need to focus our attention on a single thing, we can use different strategies to create an environment as free of distractions as possible, which encourages us to enter a flow state and do our best.

How it connects to the brain: Attention is one of our main cognitive processes that direct the brain's focus to one thing or another. However, it is limited, so we need to be smart about what we choose to pay attention to. This technique exploits the neurally based limits of our attention to allow us to focus more effectively and ensure that our brain is storing the information we want and that our focus is on the right place.

Here are the main strategies we can use to create an optimal environment that facilitates attention.

- Scheduling

One of the first causes of distraction is the lack of planning. We feel overwhelmed when we have too many things to do simultaneously. Scheduling can help us focus on a single task and know exactly how much time we have to do it (Schmidt, 2020, Distracted learning: Big problem and golden opportunity).

Planning doesn't come easy to everyone, and some struggle to be consistent with it. It's worth noting that others might have work likely to have emergencies or unplanned tasks popping up all the time. Try to create broader schedules or account for different situations, for instance, having two possible choices for a particular time depending on requirements.

You don't have to plan the day down to the most minute detail. In fact, for many, this can become more of a problem, as missing a single thing can lead to a chain reaction of missed appointments or tasks. Instead, outline your day in general terms and decide the order of the tasks to do. Allow yourself to focus on a single one at a time and deal with others as they come (Schmidt, 2020, Distracted learning: Big problem and golden opportunity).

If you are in a role or a situation when you are likely to get interrupted for other tasks or demands, for example, from other people if working at home or your colleagues in the workplace, consider leaving short spaces of time to deal with their needs or requests if they cannot be postponed.

It's also important to schedule a particular time for checking your email, phone, and messages. Don't keep notifications on all of the time. Instead, mark it as a task you will complete at one point rather than allow it to interrupt all the rest of the things you are doing. Schedule for interruptions.

Keep your schedule at hand. Some people favor digital apps or calendars, while others like a notebook or planner. What's important is that it's comfortable for you, and you can easily have it on you whenever you need to check.

If you have trouble scheduling in advance, you can focus on the next few hours or take it a day at a time. In addition, one particular variation of this is time boxing.

- Time boxing

Time boxing is a particular strategic approach to scheduling that involves allocating time boxes or periods to a particular task. During this time, all you will focus on is the task. It's a good idea to make your time boxes bigger for tasks with cognitive demands, as it allows your brain to plug into the task and reach maximum productivity through a flow state.

Time boxing involves allocating a specific period. You can use hard or soft boxes. You need to stop what you are doing with hard boxes once time runs out. With soft boxes, you might continue if there is nothing important to follow, but you note it as a stopping point. Hard boxes are better to start with when you are not used to this way of working (Eyal, 2020, Timeboxing: The Most Powerful Time Management Technique You're Probably Not Using).

It sounds very simple, but it's a good way of getting our brain to focus. You know that you will get to other tasks eventually, and an alarm can take off the pressure to watch the clock. Time boxing helps you have a clear idea of what you have to focus on and when to stop.

- Eliminating distractions

Unless you work in a sensory deprivation chamber, you really can't eliminate all distractions, which is fine. We can focus on the distractions that are the most disruptive ones.

First, we have social media, our smartphones, messengers, emails, and so on. We have mentioned that you should set a fixed time when you check your messages and emails. Otherwise, these invade the rest of your time and provide a constant stream of distraction. You can do the same with social media or your favorite sites. If you know that you will have the chance to scroll through Facebook or Instagram during lunch or at another point during the day, it becomes easier to resist the temptation to distract yourself with these.

The good idea is to turn off notifications for all your apps and messenger services. If you can, put your phone in plane mode. However, notifications that pop up on the screen or make noise are the worst offenders and immediately make us want to check them, so these should be removed (Glaveski, 2019,

Stop Letting Push Notifications Ruin Your Productivity).

Many people find it easier to avoid checking social media or the web if they are cut off completely, so the temptation is not there. There are apps and software that can block the Internet or cut off access to specific time-wasting sites and social media while allowing access to the ones you might need for work. Some are "softer" and can be turned off easily, while others are more difficult to disable.

Sometimes, a worry is that you might not see an essential message, or people will be upset that they can't reach you. Let others know when you are off the grid and leave a way of communicating with you if this is a significant concern. For example, a phone call can be distracting, but not the same way as a continuous stream of texts.

Other distractions can be harder to deal with. For example, if you are working from home, your family members might assume you are available. It's important to set boundaries. One good idea is to have a sign that marks when you should not be disturbed like a closed door or an actual do not disturb message. You can also use noise-canceling headphones or white noise and music to help you focus if you are often distracted by the sounds of other household members (Allen et al., 2020, Boundary Management and Work-Nonwork Balance While Working from Home).

Regarding your workspace, you might limit the distractions available there. Put your smartphone away and keep the things you are likely to need at hand. For instance, have a bottle of water, a pencil, or the papers you will require there. Having to get up continuously can be annoying and distracting.

Pay attention to the distractions coming from your own body. Eat a snack, drink water, stretch. These can help you stop feeling distracted faster than trying to ignore them.

- Single task at a time

Many people are used to multitasking, but as we have seen, our brain does not like this. While it might help us feel more productive, that is usually an illusion. We get more done when we go task to task (Marchewska et al., 2020, Multitasking Effects on Individual Performance: An Experimental Eye-Tracking Study).

Decide what you will focus on and commit to that one task for a specific period. If it's monotonous or boring, give yourself 15 or 25 or 45 minutes to dedicate fully to this task, and then you can move on. Often, you will finish sooner than that, but giving it your full attention ensures that you won't just do it better but that it might provide you more satisfaction.

- Using flow states

Csikszentmihalyi first described a flow state as a state that reflects a full immersion in an activity. When we are in flow, we focus on what we are doing. We are not conscious of the passage of time and might feel that little time has passed when we have been doing the task for a while. It is associated with satisfaction and engagement, and we might not be worried about anything as we do the task (Abuhamdeh, 2020, Investigating the

"Flow" Experience: Key Conceptual and Operational Issues).

Entering a flow state is a good way of ensuring our attention is directed. It also has other benefits for us. Our brains love being in flow, and it seems good for our emotional health and well-being (Abuhamdeh, 2020, Investigating the "Flow" Experience: Key Conceptual and Operational Issues).

In flow, our brains cut down on all extraneous brain activity. We stop worrying, thinking about ourselves (for example, whether we are looking silly or what we have to do tomorrow), and this leads to measurable changes in the electric activity of our neurons. Our frontal cortex works optimally and helps us make better choices and solve problems more effectively (Gold & Ciorciari, 2020, A Review on the Role of the Neuroscience of Flow States in the Modern World).

How can you enter this flow state? You have done it before when enthralled by a film, playing a game, having an exciting conversation, or many other situations. Flow happens when we find a good balance between our skills and the task's challenge. Ideally, the task is just as challenging as we need it to be, just a little above our skill level. Too much challenge or excessively high difficulty can put us off the task because of frustration. On the other hand, a task too easy evokes boredom (Gold & Ciorciari, 2020, A Review on the Role of the Neuroscience of Flow States in the Modern World).

While we are not always able to make a difficult task easier, we can divide it into smaller and more manageable chunks, reducing the difficulty level. As for tasks that are too boring, you can add more difficulty by adding something known as micro flow. It involves setting constraints (finishing in 15 minutes or doing it only with your left hand), making a game of it, or doing something at the same time, like doodling, playing with a fidget toy, or another thing that adds more stimulation to reduce boredom (Davis, 2010, Using Waiting Time Well: Toward a Theory of Microflow).

Flow is easy to sustain and very pleasant to experience. It is a state that our brain relishes and seeks, so it is likely to enhance your motivation for the tasks you know can bring it forth.

It's essential to manage our attention, and author Adam Grant suggests that it's a better idea to do this rather than just focus on managing our time. When we can pay full attention, our brain works best, but multitasking is akin to self-sabotage, and, what's more insidious, we can't always tell just how much distractions affect us.

Flaws in our thinking: cognitive biases

So, we can't pay attention to more than one thing at a time, at least, not without having to pay costs in terms of outcomes and accomplishments. And yet, most people believe that they can multitask successfully, with some feeling more productive when they have various things going on simultaneously. This suggests that we don't have an intrinsic awareness of the things best for our brain or our performance.

This is an issue that many cognitive scientists have recognized. When we make decisions or judge a situation, we rarely know exactly why we arrive at a particular conclusion or why we see things in a certain way. Cognitive bias comes in to explain why this happens.

A cognitive bias is a mistake in thinking or making decisions we all are prone to making at some point. These are typical errors that can lead to worse outcomes, and they are associated with the way our brain functions.

Neural networks have association as their central property, and the brain likes to find patterns in information to combine them. Regarding cognitive information, this can lead to distortions. For example, we might be likely to recognize coincidences as a pattern and act accordingly, leading us to superstitious behaviors (and not just humans, even pigeons' brains have the same processing flaw). Our brains might make associations that are inaccurate (Korteling, Brower, & Toet, 2018, A Neural Network Framework for Cognitive Bias).

For example, imagine that you did not take an umbrella with you, and it rained. Logically, there is no connection, but you might remember other times this has happened and conclude that it will rain whenever you don't take an umbrella.

This is a relatively innocuous example. In other cases, bias can lead to significant harm. For example, many gamblers fall prey to the so-called gambler's fallacy and make losing bets. Bias can make us hire a worse candidate while ignoring a better one for a job, make a bad financial decision that will make us feel guilty and have a real cost, or trust a person that will trick us.

Let's consider some of the most common cognitive biases.

- Halo effect

The halo effect involves us judging a person more negatively or more positively based on a single characteristic, usually attractiveness. We tend to perceive more attractive people as smarter, more capable, and more knowledgeable (Talamas, Mavor, & Perett, 2016, Blinded by Beauty: Attractiveness Bias and

Accurate Perceptions of Academic Performance).

- Misinformation effect

The misinformation effect is a bias where receiving new and inaccurate information after a situation can change our memory and perception of the situation itself, even if we know the information was false (Challies, Hunt, Garry, & Harper, 2016, Whatever Gave You That Idea? False Memories Following Equivalence Training: A Behavioral Account of the Misinformation Effect).

- Anchoring effect

The anchoring effect involves our judgment being affected by any information we received beforehand, even unrelated. For example, if a person sees a large number and then gets to look at a price tag for a product, they are more likely to see it as a fair or low price. Their judgment is influenced by having seen a large number, even if it had nothing to do with the product's price (Furnham & Boo, 2011, A literature review of the anchoring effect).

- Bandwagon effect

We prefer things that are popular or, rather, those that we see as being more popular. This can apply to political candidates, shows, opinions, and anything else that seems more attractive if it seems favored by the majority (Barnfield, 2019, Think Twice before Jumping on the Bandwagon: Clarifying Concepts in Research on the Bandwagon Effect).

- Familiarity bias

We usually prefer things familiar to us. When we choose, we favor the brands or products we already know over new ones. This can go beyond product choice to political decisions or life choices that show a preference for the status quo (Blanchard, 2016, Familiarity Bias: Examining a Cognitive-Affective Mechanism Underlying Ideological Support for the Status Quo).

These are just a few examples. There are many more cognitive biases out there, and we are all subject to their effects. The truly interesting thing is that we are not aware of these biases or their impact. If asked why we chose one thing over another, we are unlikely to say: "Oh, the person who sold it to me was attractive. Clearly, this means that they were more competent." But the effect remains without us knowing it.

Cognitive biases are byproducts of our usually efficient and effective brain and its way of dealing with situations that threaten our survival. We can't be fully rid of these biases (and believing we are bias-free is another bias), but we can learn about them and account for them to make better decisions.

Technique #3: Structuring your decisions

It matters little whether you pick orange or apple juice based on your bias. If you choose a workplace or even a career, it matters a lot using this as a guide. Pay special attention to the decisions associated with significant consequences for yourself and others around you.

How it connects to the brain: Our brain structures thinking and decision-making processes in a particular way that works most of the time. However, it also leads to cognitive biases, which are common to all of us and can be seen as persistent bugs in our reasoning. They can lead us astray in important choices, which makes it important to know how to neutralize their effects and make our decisions better and stronger. We cannot eliminate our biases because they are intrinsic to our brain's functioning, so learning about them and reducing their effect is the best choice.

Here is where you can structure your decisions.

- Recognize that you might be susceptible to bias

The first step is very simple. Recognize that you might make biased choices even if you feel objective. Your brain operates in specific ways that are good for your survival, but have side effects. If you account for them, you can improve your outcomes. Even if something feels natural and evident, it might not be so from an objective viewpoint.

- Consider the opposite

Consider the opposite is a cognitive strategy that asks you to think of any reasons your initial judgment might be wrong, even if it feels right. Ask yourself if there are way you might be inaccurate and make an honest attempt to engage with the question (Korteling, Gerritsma, & Toet, 2021, Retention and Transfer of Cognitive Bias Mitigation Interventions: A Systematic Literature Study).

- Seek contrary perspectives, evidence, and opinions

It's easy to find information aligned with our opinions (confirmation bias), but we might need opposing information. This can be more useful, even if it generates frustration. Make a conscious effort to consider information that goes against what you believe to be true. Are the sources reliable? Can you see why someone might believe things contrary to your opinion?

This doesn't mean you must change your opinion all the time. But contrary information can make your perspective more nuanced and effective. Ask advice from contrarians and bring in those who will have a different perspective, whether because of their background or other factors (Wolf, 2012, How to Minimize Your Biases When Making Decisions).

- Reframe the problem

We take an overly negative or positive view of any situation. One way of addressing bias is to flip the situation around. Find the negatives in a good situation and the positives in a bad one. It can help you get a more detailed understanding and makes your mind more flexible (Wolf, 2012, How to Minimize Your Biases When Making Decisions).

- Don't commit too soon

Sometimes, we realize that we have made a mistake, but we have committed to our choice. Don't make public announcements, and don't tell people until you are certain, especially in complicated situations. Social pressure can make you dig in even if you learn on some level that your decision was influenced by bias.

- Speed and stress don't help

Take your time with complex decisions. When we have to make them under pressure, feeling anxious or tired or rushed, we are more susceptible to bias, and our brain uses the bias to make quicker choices. We can't always avoid pressure, but taking a few moments to think and breathe in and out can help us make a more rational choice (Korteling, Gerritsma, & Toet, 2021, Retention and Transfer of Cognitive Bias Mitigation Interventions: A Systematic Literature Study).

- Use objective measures

Sometimes, a good solution is to develop objective measures to determine whether your decision succeeded. Involve checklists, outside observers, and other tools that will help you reduce the impact of bias (Wolf, 2012, How to Minimize Your Biases When Making Decisions).

Our identity improves our habits

Do you think of yourself as an athlete? Maybe as a gamer or as an entrepreneur or an activist? The question of our identity is very significant.

Our brain likes having things that are clear cut and can fit in specific categories. We group the people around us and ourselves in groups. When we feel like we belong to a group, we tend to value the characteristics associated with the group. We get defensive if we attack this part of our identity and view outsiders with suspicion (Abbink & Harris, 2019, In-group favoritism and out-group discrimination in naturally occurring groups). The in-group and out-group biases are powerful and can contribute to negative situations, like exclusion or discrimination or in-group favoritism. But we can turn this tendency around to achieve better results.

Technique #4 Shifting your group identity

When we link our identity to our habits and everyday practices, it becomes easier to sustain them. Our identity is the narrative we tell ourselves about who we are and who we want to be. It impacts our choices and behaviors: what we do and what we avoid, what type of values we hold and how they manifest in daily life (Verplanken & Sui, 2019, Habit and Identity: Behavioral, Cognitive, Affective, and Motivational Facets of an Integrated Self).

How it connects to the brain: Our brains are deeply oriented towards social motivation. Being rejected, for example, hurts just as much as physical pain and occurs in the same brain circuits (Kross et al., 2011, Social rejection shares somatosensory representations with physical pain).

Identities are also connected to groups. For instance, if we are part of a movement, we might feel more inclined to give the movement money, participate in their protests, and endorse their values. Our behavior changes if we suddenly have a "break-up" with the cause.

Here is an example. A person who belongs to a casual group of friends who get together in bars to drink might engage in drinking and smoking with their friends. This might even become a habit. But if they join a group of fitness fans who jog and drink smoothies, the person might slowly shift the habit of drinking. They will adopt new habits to better fit with their new crew and a better fit with their new identity as a person who cares about their health, exercises, etc. Our brain does not like the state of dissonance that appears when our values and actions don't match and is very concerned with belonging, so we are more likely to be motivated to fit with our new identity.

The technique involves two aspects. First, it can involve finding a group that fits the values and lifestyle habits you want to have. The second is to build a conscious link between this new identity and the habits you will develop every day.

- Find a community that lives your values

It's easier to exercise if you surround yourself with people who exercise, talk about fitness and health, and who can support your initiative. This works on several levels. First, joining a group like this can give you access to advice and new experiences that can sustain your new habits. Second, it can motivate you to be more like the people around you, not just to fit in better, though this can be a good reason, but also because you will learn from them and be influenced by their practices (Sani, 2012, Group identification, social relationships, and health). It's something our social brain is very, very good at.

Does this mean that it's time to break up with all the friends who smoke and watch TV? Not really. Social support and close relationships matter too. However, building new connections with new people can help to shift to a new habit. You might spend less time with the friends whose lifestyle and habits are very contrary to your goals and immerse yourself more intensely into the new group or culture. Just make sure that you feel comfortable with this group and that it does not offer toxic practices, for example, in the case of exercise, unhealthy diets or steroid use.

- Attach the identity to yourself

Saying that you're a smoker shows an entirely different level of commitment to the behavior than saying you are someone who smokes. This also applies to healthy habits. Saying you are a non-smoker can help you avoid cigarettes because this avoidance becomes a part of your identity (Sani, 2012, Group identification, social relationships, and health).

Sometimes, we start with an aspirational label, e.g., saying you are a non-smoker even if you could not fully give up cigarettes. That's OK. Imagine your ideal self - the version of you that has accomplished this. It's aspirational. When tempted or confused, ask yourself: what would a non-smoker do? What would my ideal self do in this situation?

This is a way to make better choices and sustain them. It motivates you to keep going, and identity labels have a powerful effect on our brain. We can see it in many situations, and our brain falls for it a lot. A company like Apple, for example, builds a large aspect of its branding around the idea that using their products is not just a consumer choice. It's an identity choice. People who use Apple products are different. And it works! You can even see the in-group and out-group conflict between Apple and Android users, as it has become about more than just a phone brand. It's about identity and belonging to a group.

Our brain is not perfect. It can make poor choices and is very driven by a host of tricky biases, especially those we are unaware of. Our attention can be limited, and we can sometimes fall into bad habits or the tendency to let our desire for identity and belonging derail us. But when we gain this awareness, we can turn these situations to our advantage. Think of it this way: the brain's flaws and strengths are sometimes the same. The brain wants to save energy, create shortcuts and make life easier, but these tendencies can backfire and cause us to be lazy, habitual and biased. However, none of this is a problem if we maintain awareness and creatively work around our tendencies and limitations.

Takeaways

- Improving our lives is difficult primarily because we lack the knowledge of how to do so and the right tools. But it's also intrinsically difficult because of our brain's natural weaknesses and flaws.

- We can use scientifically proven general strategies for helping us achieve our goals, given our brain's drawbacks.
- One issue is that we cannot force our way out of acquired habit by willpower alone, and we cannot use neural connections that simply aren't there. But we can build connections with every repetition until it becomes automatic. Behaviors consist of triggers, routines and rewards. We can work with this habit loop and re-engineer the habits we already have, so the desired behavior becomes easy and automatic – with time! Consistency is key.
- Brains have limited attentional capacity, and multitasking comes with a switching cost. We can tweak our environment to make the most of our attention and be more productive: we can fine-tune our scheduling strategy, use "time-boxing" and cut down on distractions. It's easier to get into a "flow state" when we focus on one task at a time without distraction.
- Cognitive biases are distortions in our judgments and perceptions, and can undermine our ability to think clearly, especially if they're unconscious. To make more objective decisions, acknowledge

that you may be susceptible to bias, seek contrary perspectives, reframe the problem and don't act in haste.
- Finally, we can use our need for identity to support good habit formation by seeking communities with shared values and deliberately attaching that identity to ourselves.

Chapter 3. Peak Performance and Executive Functioning

There are innate, natural patterns that our brain has followed for thousands of years. Even if they are constantly challenged and undermined in the modern world, deep down, the brain is still running on cognitive routines, preferences and programs that took our entire shared history to evolve. Let's dig into some important biological aspects of our neural functioning, and how we can work with rather than against them.

Follow the rhythm

Our bodies follow a specific biological pattern that determines states of alertness and sleepiness, hunger and satiation, and more. The body has a clock that determines different the timing of aspects of our behavior and sensations. Like everything else, this clock is tied to our brain (Laje, Agostino, & Golombek, 2018, The Times of Our Lives: Interaction Among Different Biological Periodicities).

The clock marks the biological rhythms, i.e. the natural cycles of change of the brain chemicals and hormones. A master clock coordinates other clocks across the body, and the master clock is in the brain. The clocks need to be synchronized, and some things, like jet lag or chronic sleep deprivation, can throw them out of whack (Laje, Agostino, & Golombek, 2018, The Times of Our Lives: Interaction Among Different Biological Periodicities).

The human experience is coordinated across several biological rhythms. First, circadian rhythms refer to the 24-hour cycle and the changes within this period. For example, before we feel sleepy, our bodies release melatonin to produce the sensation, and thus we're prompted to want to sleep at predictable times every day. When we wake, our brain signals cortisol release, which gets us up and moving. This signal depends on cues from the environment and specialized cells that literally sense the passage of time and orchestrate behavior accordingly.

Another type of rhythm is called ultradian; these rhythms are shorter than 24 hours and include things like pulse, breathing rate, appetite, blink rate and REM sleep cycles, which last around 90 minutes. Finally, there are infradian rhythms longer than 24 hours, such as migration, hair growth, or menstruation (Laje, Agostino, & Golombek, 2018, The Times of Our Lives: Interaction Among Different Biological Periodicities).

If you're thinking about habit, performance and changing behavior, it's wise to consider how the body naturally organizes its behavior. It's all about timing: an obvious example is not to force yourself to learn something new and complicated at 2am, when everything in your body is priming your brain to sleep. When we understand our rhythms, we can schedule things more effectively and can also take care to keep our clocks running on time. Let's consider each rhythm and how we might maintain them to improve our lives.

Technique #5 Planning according to our brain clock

The first aspect of this technique involves *observing* your natural rhythms. You can't make changes until you know realistically what you're dealing with. Pick several 24-hour cycles, preferably on days that are average for you and don't involve any particular changes in your sleep or eating cycles or any extraordinary levels of stress. Choose at least one weekday and a day on the weekend.

Observe and write down the times when you feel most alert and awake. What time do you wake up normally when you don't have to wake up at a specific time? What time do you wake up if you have gotten enough sleep? Note the times when you feel most and least productive. Usually, our alertness will spike throughout the day, rising and dropping. Some people are especially productive in the morning, while others do their best in the evening or the afternoon or even during the night.

Note when is the best time to go to bed and wake up. If you know the times when you are most productive, you can schedule the most difficult and demanding tasks for these hours of the day.

How it connects to the brain: Our brain has a master clock that controls our biological rhythms. This clock runs to its own rhythm - we can't thrive if we ignore it. Understanding this and organizing our life according to this rhythm can make us more productive and happier as well.

When considering your schedule, you might discover your chronotype. A chronotype is a pattern of sleep and productivity spikes that focus on specific times. You might have heard about the lark and the owl: people who are most productive in the morning and in the evening/night, respectively. However, other chronotypes have been identified by Dr. Breus (2016, The Power of When) who presents a clear outline of four main types and suggests a productivity cycle for each. These types are more specific than the lark/owl division. They are believed to be based in biology, specifically, on gene expression and brain functioning, so it's difficult to change one's chronotype. Instead, it can be best to try and adapt our lifestyle to it.

- Bear

Most people, around 55%, belong to the bear chronotype. They follow the solar cycle: getting up at 7 am and going to bed at 11 pm. Their productivity spikes between 10 am and 2 pm and drops after lunch.

- Wolf

Wolves sleep best between 12 am and 7 am. Their productivity spikes between 5 pm and 12 am. Around 15% of people fit in this chronotype.

- Lion

Lions sleep best between 10 pm and 6 am. Their focus and productivity go up between 8 am and 12 pm, so they are the most clear-cut "morning" type.

- Dolphin

Around 10% of the population are dolphins. Dolphins rest best between 11:30 pm and 6:30 am. Their best productivity time is between 3 and 9 pm.

Discovering your chronotype can help you decide how to schedule your tasks. For example, Bears and Lions can start with their heaviest tasks, while Dolphins do better if they can build up their more difficult tasks by starting with the easier ones.

Use your chronotype to make a schedule optimal for you. You might note that the chronotypes still do better if they go to bed at midnight, and this is associated with another brain characteristic: we rest better if we go to sleep between 10 pm and 2 am and get enough sleep, no matter who we are or what our chronotype is (Walker, 2017, Why We Sleep).

Despite each having our own chronotype, our internal clocks can be disrupted by different things. Our brains use light as one of the main signals, but eating and physical activity, as well as a disrupted and inconsistent sleep schedule, can also mess with our internal configuration. A good idea is to avoid bright light as your bedtime approaches and increase natural light exposure in the mornings. Avoid heavy meals and physical activity before bed (Walker, 2017, Why We Sleep).

This concerns circadian rhythms, the 24-hour cycle we experience every day. But what about ultradian and infradian cycles?

Ultradian cycles are shorter than 24 hours. Since the 1950s, it has been suggested that our brains and, as a result, our bodies, move through 90 to 120 minutes cycle when we are awake and asleep. They define how our alertness might ebb and flow. Our attention will rise and fall during this time, as will our energy. When our bodies are at their best and we feel full of energy, we can take advantage to get things done and schedule our breaks for the ebb of our alertness (Goh, Maloney, Mark, & Blanche, 2019, Episodic Ultradian Events—Ultradian Rhythms).

We might push against these cycles to a degree, but this can lead to significant issues in the long term. When we look at the top performers across fields, such as a classic study done with young violin players, we can find they adapt their practice and performance to these cycles. They tend to work for 60 to 90 minutes and take breaks later, alternating between intense work bursts and recovery (Ericsson, Krampe, & Tesh-Romero, 1993, The Role of Deliberate Practice in the Acquisition of Expert Performance). This means that it's not useful to plan to work for several hours straight with no distractions. Instead, focus on alternating between intense work and rest within the cycle. It can feel counterintuitive and even lazy, but the results are likely to be better than you might get if you are pushing yourself to work harder and harder.

Infradian rhythms regarding a monthly cycle can be more relevant for women than for men, as women must pay more attention to their menstrual cycles and hormonal changes. For women, planning for their infradian cycles can be useful, as it allows them to allocate less work for specific days and do more intense work on other weeks (Schechter, 2010, Sleep, Hormones, and Circadian Rhythms throughout the Menstrual Cycle in Healthy

Women and Women with Premenstrual Dysphoric Disorder).

However, infradian cycles might cover even a year. Many people find that their energy dips in winter, for example, when there is less sunlight, and prepare themselves by taking more vitamins or planning for the biggest projects they have to take place over the spring and summer months. Winter and autumn can lead to seasonal affective disorder or seasonal depression (Melrose, 2015, Seasonal Affective Disorder: An Overview of Assessment and Treatment Approaches).

Our brain controls our internal clocks, and our basic schedule appears to be rooted in biology. This means that adapting to it and taking it into account is a better strategy than forcing a change.

Our brain likes fun and easy: why we procrastinate

Procrastination affects most of us at some point. Around 80 to 95% of individuals report procrastinating at some time (Novotney, 2010, Procrastination or 'intentional delay'?). The rest, perhaps, do the same but do not report it! We are all likely to face putting things off. We are likely to put off important things as well, and even more so. Big projects that require an early start often get put off until the last minute, even if it rationally makes no sense.

Your brain is big on saving energy and effort. It wants to find the simplest, easiest and most pleasurable way through a task – why wouldn't it? But our brains are also not rational, and procrastination is a clear example of this. Often, we might perceive the task we have to do as difficult, unpleasant, challenging, or boring. We might know that it must be done right away and that putting it off will only bring trouble. Yet, we often cannot bring ourselves to do what needs to be done. Why?

One issue tied to procrastination is choosing to do what is necessary but hard instead of what is unnecessary but is easy, fun, or pleasant. Our brain often will pursue instant gratification - an activity that promises an immediate reward are perceived as more attractive. Delaying gratification is an important skill to reach success. We can do it often until suddenly we find ourselves procrastinating on something that has a huge impact on our success, health, or relationships. Why does this happen?

We can prefer instant gratification more when tired, stressed, or experiencing negative emotions. Our willpower drops. It can also be a more likely outcome when we perceive the task as too intimidating, too dull, too complex, or a challenge to our ability. If we are afraid of failing or doing a bad job, we might also avoid the task due to perfectionism. Instant gratification becomes much more difficult to resist when we don't want to do the task we have to complete (Moshin & Ayub, 2014, The relationship between procrastination, delay of gratification, and job satisfaction among high school teachers).

We can work with motivation and resolve our perfectionism, but one of the easiest tactics to reduce procrastination is to tap into our brain's search for instant gratification. By changing the way we perceive the task, we motivate ourselves to do it right away and reduce procrastination.

Technique #6 Making a task more attractive for our brain

It will take enormous amounts of energy and effort to use sheer willpower to tackle procrastination. But driving home how unpleasant and mandatory a task is will likely only lessen its appeal, making it harder to do! Instead, we can work *with* our brain's preference for easy and pleasurable things, and use different strategies to make a task more appealing, such as reducing it to smaller tasks that do not seem that intimidating or reframing it more positively. However, here we will talk about how we can make a task appear more fun and the different ways to help our brain get more interested in it.

How it appeals to the brain: We have a highly developed motivation/reward system mainly drawn to things that aid our survival and that promise to engage our dopaminergic system. Games and fun activities that seem easy to finish and get a result to draw us in consistently.

If we can make the tasks that bore and frustrate us seem more like the things our brain likes, it is certain to provide enough dopamine to take our motivation higher.

- Extrinsic motivation: rewards

Extrinsic motivation boils down to rewards and punishments for completing our tasks. You'll recall from the habit loop that rewards reinforce the routine that came before and makes it more likely to occur. Rewards tend to show better results than punishments and fewer negative effects as well (Pink, 2009, Drive: The Surprising Truth About What Motivates Us). This strategy is as simple as making a reward conditioned on completing the task.

Rewards are not the most effective way of doing this, but they can create a good incentive for a short-term, dull task, like filing your taxes or running an errand. It is better to use them for something that is a one-time thing and not for something that can become a habit, as rewards seem to lose their effectiveness when used continuously (Pink, 2009, Drive: The Surprising Truth About

What Motivates Us). Our brains like surprises and novel rewards, but the shine wears off quickly, and we are not as eager to get things done for a prize, so this is best used sparingly.

Make your reward something enjoyable, and don't stick to material rewards. A fun experience can be as good as a treat or a purchase. Try to avoid situations where you can easily access the reward before completing the task and commit to making it conditional on task completion. Also avoid rewards that undo the benefit of the task!

- Intrinsic motivation: autonomy, belonging, mastery, and purpose

Intrinsic motivation seems more complex than extrinsic motivation. It involves a strong link to dopaminergic systems. Dopamine is one of the main neurotransmitters for our brain, one involved with the feeling of satisfaction, curiosity, the desire to seek and do more (Di Domenico & Ryan, 2017, The Emerging Neuroscience of Intrinsic Motivation: A New Frontier in Self-Determination Research). It's fun to get a treat or a prize, but this is not usually enough for some tasks, especially for the long term. Employers discover this frequently: they can only do so much to incentivize workers before they start needing a more genuine and meaningful reason for doing something. When intrinsic motivation becomes involved, we get a stronger pleasure boost with more lasting motivation. We are not just making temporary behavior changes, but we are experiencing the deeper internal shifts accompanying real transformation.

As the name suggests, intrinsic motivation comes from within and involves emotional experiences like curiosity, pride, fun, social connection, and others. According to the main framework for understanding it, four things engage our brain more and keep it hooked via increases in intrinsic motivation.

Autonomy is the first element. We are more motivated to do things we get to decide about. Even a boring task becomes more interesting when we have more freedom to choose when or how we do it. Increasing your autonomy over a task can help you feel more motivated to do it, so add your own touch to the process or the outcome (Pink, 2009, Drive: The Surprising Truth About What Motivates Us).

The second element is belonging. When something brings us into contact with other people, it becomes more desirable for our brain to pursue social connections. Consider whether you can bring someone else to support you with the task or use it to further your connections or relationships. Tie a dull errand to meeting a friend, for instance, or find an accountability partner (Pink, 2009, Drive: The Surprising Truth About What Motivates Us).

The third element is mastery. Mastery is the desire to be better and further our skills. Even if the task itself is undesirable or mundane, can you frame it as a task that will allow your personal or professional growth? Can you connect it with a particular goal or skill you would like to promote (Pink, 2009, Drive: The Surprising Truth About What Motivates Us)?

The fourth element of intrinsic motivation is purpose or meaning. Why are you doing the task? What is its deeper purpose? How does it connect to your values or ideals? What is the point of doing it? Some types of work are particularly meaningless by themselves but might help if you reframe them in terms of the value they bring to you or your community. The goal is to connect with the meaning of the work you are doing and trying to enjoy it or, at least, to recognize why it must be done beyond a more superficial reason (Pink, 2009, Drive: The Surprising Truth About What Motivates Us).

- Gamification

Our brains love games and game-like activities. They promise instant gratification and fun, so what's not to enjoy? Marketers and professionals from other areas have recognized the power that games have to motivate us, which helped create the practice of gamification - making different activities more like games by introducing different elements. You have seen examples of this approach in different apps, such as a progress bar, achievements, points, and other elements borrowed from games. We can use gamification by making boring or challenging tasks more similar to games and engaging our dopamine release systems to motivate us more strongly to avoid procrastination (McGonigal, 2015, SuperBetter: A Revolutionary Approach to Getting Stronger, Happier, Braver and More Resilient).

How can you employ gamification? Here are a few ideas. You can treat tasks throughout the day as minigames that yield points. Once you reach a specific number of points, you get a reward or level up. Focus on them as challenges you pass to gain more experience or unlock the next task (Patel, 2019, Gamify Your Life and Become Massively Successful).

You can use narrative or role-playing. Visualize yourself as a secret agent completing an assignment or an alien trying to blend in. Imagine why this task has high stakes and how it fits within a story that casts you as the hero.

Some apps and tools help you gamify your life, such as Habitica and SuperBetter. If you employ them, you get a predetermined structure that tricks your brain into thinking you are playing a game as your goals are accomplished faster and more successfully.

Games are a dopamine goldmine. Applying these strategies to other areas of our life can help our brain feel more motivated and willing to do any tasks without procrastination.

Disengaging your brain's autopilot

When we talked about routines, we mentioned that creating habits can save your brain some energy. You don't have to think consciously or even engage with many habits, like brushing your teeth or cleaning your kitchen, and that's a very useful thing. It saves much effort and allows our brain to focus on other things instead, hopefully, something that brings more value. But this autopilot can be engaged in other situations where it hurts more than it helps.

Our brain has regions that activate when we are not engaged consciously with the outside world, for example, when daydreaming or remembering or picturing the future. This is called the default mode network. In addition to these situations, this is also the active brain network when doing a familiar task or disconnected from an experience.

The default mode network can be good for situations when performing a familiar task or are in a familiar environment. However, there are other issues with it. Sometimes, we miss chunks of time when our brain's DMN is active. We miss experiences and details, and we are not operating at our best. Autopilot can lead to us missing experiences and making mistakes if the situation changes without us being aware of it (Vatansever, Menon, & Samakatis, 2017, Default mode contributions to automated information processing).

One of the main effects of an overactive DMN is the sensation that time is going by too fast (and not in the nice, flow-state way) but that nothing is happening. We might describe this experience as being stuck in a routine where every day is the same. We don't notice where our days are going, mostly, and feel that nothing is happening. This suggests that we are running on autopilot.

We want the autopilot for habits and such to save energy. But when it begins to run most of the time, it's like we are absent from most of our life. This can be true for people who have somewhat repetitive tasks and functions, and all of us might feel something similar. It brings down our productivity, performance, and overall satisfaction.

But how can we kick our brains into gear and counteract the effects of the DMN so it doesn't end up running throughout the day?

Technique #7 Novelty as an antidote to the default mode network

The neuroplasticity of your brain helps it adapt to the current situation. If you do the same thing every day, if you live through a routine, then the brain adapts to it and usually does it by relying more on the default mode network because it makes sense. But this means we can use neuroplasticity again to our advantage and turn off the state of disconnection.

How it connects to the brain: Our brain likes saving energy in the default mode network. It is also shaped by neuroplasticity to adjust to its current environment and behave in ways that make sense for that environment. Constant routines and lack of novelty make the brain engage the DMN more frequently.

Novelty and changes in our environment that defy expectations switch the default mode network off to manual mode, because we have to pay attention and react. Here is where novelty can help us significantly to improve our engagement with daily situations.

- Novel skills

Learning new skills is a good way of adding novelty to our lives and has the distinct advantage of growing other abilities. Language learning is one of the best skills we can use, as it can also enhance our neuroplasticity and take our brain's abilities to the next level (Bubbico et al., 2019, Effects of Second Language Learning on the Plastic Aging Brain: Functional Connectivity, Cognitive Decline, and Reorganization).

Learning any new skills is good for the brain and pushes us to pay attention. It maintains interest and offers a way to enhance our experiences further. If we learn a new language, we might gain access to a whole new set of literature, film, and culture, for example, all brimming with novelty, or even to a new field of work or ways to grow professionally and reach positions that require creativity and less routine.

- Do normal tasks in an unusual way

You can add novelty and train your brain by performing tasks in new ways. The easiest strategy here is to shift from your dominant hand to your non-dominant hand for tooth brushing, writing, or another mundane activity. Do it in a new setting or using different tools. Don't do all your work this way, but switching it up for some mundane tasks can push your brain to pay attention. Besides this, it might stimulate the corpus callosum - the connecting tissue between both hemispheres of your brain (Stockel and Weitgel, 2012, Brain lateralization and motor learning: selective effects of dominant and non-dominant hand practice on the early acquisition of throwing skills). If you always write in your notebook vertically, try writing horizontally. However, such small changes barely require more time can stimulate your attention networks and disconnect the DMN.

- Make a single novel choice

You might remember that your brain favors the familiar over the novel due to a cognitive bias. You will probably pick similar dishes for lunch or go to places you know. However, a good way to cut down on the routine is to commit to making one choice in favor of novelty. Try a new dessert or food you have never had before. Take a different route from work or take a walk in an unfamiliar area. Go see a film of a genre you usually avoid. Little bits of novelty can encourage your brain to engage with the situation and experience it more deeply, and they help shut off the autopilot (Dean, 2019, The Importance of Novelty).

- Play games and solve puzzles

An easy way to add novelty and stimulate our brain is to add a few games and puzzles here and there. You can try mobile apps, video games, brain training programs, and many other ways of accessing them. Games can help keep your brain stimulated and are an easy way to discover new experiences, available even when tired or stuck at home. Games put demands on your brain, which trains some abilities, and can also improve your overall cognitive health in addition to cutting down on the DMN's functioning (Fissler, Kolassa, & Schreder, 2015, Educational games for brain health: revealing their unexplored potential through a neurocognitive approach). Not all games are made equal - find something challenging rather than too easy, but not frustratingly difficult either.

A little novelty can reduce the sensation that you are absent from your life and renew your energy, curiosity, and motivation. But we can use neuroplasticity even more to work on some of the central skills that underlie essentially everything we do, our decisions, and our ability to succeed professionally and in our relationships.

Investing time into executive skills

You might remember that your brain has four lobes. The frontal lobe behind your forehead plays a significant role in our daily lives. It is the control center for all our higher-order functions, such as morality, emotional regulation, and decision-making. It is the area associated with executive skills.

Executive skills are those that allow us to exert fine control over our behavior, cut down on impulsive behavior, and avoid decisions that might be good in the short-term but bad in the long term, like gambling all your money away or fighting a man who just insulted you in a bar. Good executive skills are associated with greater success at work, academic contexts, and relationships. Someone with poor executive skills can be visualized as an impulsive person with difficulties controlling and expressing their emotions and problems solving issues by combining information or remembering what they know (Blair, 2017, Developmental Science and Executive Function).

One of the most dramatic cases of executive dysfunction was the case of Phineas Gage, a 19th century railroad worker. By all accounts, Gage was a reliable worker and a family man until he suffered a terrible accident one day. A metal rod was projected through his skull and went straight through his frontal lobes. Gage survived and recovered, but his personality suffered a dramatic shift. Instead of the reliable foreman, he was now an irresponsible, irascible, and profane man reported to behave like an animal, drinking and swearing. He did a complete personality turn due to the damage his frontal lobes received and the damage to his executive functions (Ardila, 2018).

On the other hand, improved executive functions are associated with success across different areas. We can find evidence that young soccer players (Vestberg et al., 2017, Core executive functions are associated with success in young elite soccer players) and high school students (Diamond, 2014, Want to Optimize Executive Functions and Academic Outcomes? Simple, Just Nourish the Human Spirit), marital harmony and the ability to get and keep a job (Diamond, 2014, Want to Optimize Executive Functions and Academic Outcomes? Simple, Just Nourish the Human Spirit; Eakin et al., 2004, The marital and family functioning of adults with ADHD and their spouses), and a healthier lifestyle, are all tied to higher executive functioning.

Thanks to neuroplasticity, we can improve these skills and achieve significant gains across different areas of our lives. Even if we start more impulsive, for instance, we have the power to rewire the brain. So, let's focus on each executive skill in turn and see what we can do to boost this neurological ability and train our frontal cortex to do its job with more efficiency.

The number one skill is self-control. Self-control or inhibitory control is the ability to resist the pull of stimuli like emotions, habits, and external distractions and the ability to keep our behavior, attention, thoughts, and emotions focused where we want them. The ability allows us to resist impulsive actions and avoid temptations that could harm us. Self-control is tied to values and skills like perseverance and discipline (Diamond, 2014, Want to Optimize Executive Functions and Academic Outcomes? Simple, Just Nourish the Human Spirit).

How it connects to the brain: Our executive skills, in particular, self-control, are connected to specific areas of the brain. By practicing them so it reinforces the functioning of this area, we can make real change regarding our functioning and make our brain operate differently with basic skills that influence a wide variety of areas in our lives.

Technique #8 Training our self-control

Self-control is not always the easiest skill to have. It's worth remembering that our brain might be more vulnerable to temptation when there is a lot of stress, fatigue, and negative emotion. Some situations can get the best of us. Many feel they do not have enough self-control to resist that one treat or throw a comment that might escalate the situation. But we can train this ability like a muscle.

- Meditation

Meditation is touted to solve different problems, and self-control is not the exception. Meditation is proven to rewire our brains quickly and with cumulative effects the more we practice. Self-regulation can improve with meditation practice, a result seen with kids under five, undergraduate students, and participants over 65 years, which suggests that it's a practice with broad effects. Meditation seems to improve activation and connectivity in areas of the brain connected to self-regulation (Tang, Posner, & Rothbart, 2014, Meditation improves self-regulation over the life span).

Meditation is easy to practice and has proven effects on the brain. Just like taxi drivers were able to make their hippocampus bigger because of their training, meditation can enhance and build the areas of the brain related to self-regulation (Tang, Posner, & Rothbart, 2014, Meditation improves self-regulation over the life span; Maguire et al., 2000, Navigation-related structural change in the hippocampi of taxi drivers).

There is robust evidence suggesting that mindfulness meditation is a good way of increasing self-regulation. Some effects become evident after only five days of practice (Tang, Posner, & Rothbart, 2014, Meditation improves self-regulation over the life span). But most forms of meditation use the same principles.

Meditation involves becoming aware of the present moment and focusing our attention on the present or a specific thing, like a mantra or a thought or an idea. Mindfulness meditation, in particular, involves focusing on the present moment and allowing one's sensations and thoughts come and go without judgment, without engaging with them. This helps us become more conscious of what we think and how we think and control our negative thoughts and experiences. During meditation, you can focus on your breathing or on the sensations of your body (Behan, 2020, The benefits of meditation and mindfulness practices during times of crisis, such as COVID-19).

The specific changes associated with meditation involve increased activity in the prefrontal cortex and lower activity in the amygdala, which indicates a lower emotional activation and better self-regulation. The more you practice meditation, the more these changes become intrinsic to your neural architecture (Behan, 2020, The benefits of meditation and mindfulness practices during times of crisis, such as COVID-19).

Meditation is easy enough to start with. Even if you find your mind and awareness wandering, you are still meditating and still getting the benefits as long as you try to focus. The effort is likely to yield additional benefits for self-regulation and rewire your brain for better control of yourself and reduced impulsivity.

- Resisting temptation

Resisting temptation is easier said than done. We can train our self-control muscle by resisting the pull to do something that is not good for us. However, we can also try to add strategies for delaying gratification to better cope with any temptation that comes our way rather than just attempting to push back against the desire.

We can use various strategies to enhance our self-control, so we need not rely on willpower alone. This is strategy number 1: using willpower to just not do the thing. But sometimes, the temptation might be too big, or we might feel too tired. So, what other strategies do we have at our disposal (Milyavskaya, Saunders, & Inzlicht, 2020, Self-control in daily life: Prevalence and effectiveness of diverse self-control strategies)?

Walking away from the situation or removing the temptation is an effective strategy in many cases. If the snacks tempt you, leave the kitchen or put them away into the pantry. To go and surf online before bed, move the phone away (Milyavskaya, Saunders, & Inzlicht, 2020, Self-control in daily life: Prevalence and effectiveness of diverse self-control strategies).

The next strategy is to distract yourself. Focus on something else, preferably something that will be fun or involving. Get busy doing work or learning or playing or listening to music. Find an effective distraction that is enjoyable and interesting on its own (Milyavskaya, Saunders, & Inzlicht, 2020, Self-control in daily life: Prevalence and effectiveness of diverse self-control strategies).

Another strategy is to connect with your goals or why you want to resist. Is it bad for you? How is it bad? What is the goal you are pursuing now by resisting? Is there a reason you are doing this? This is a strategy that can help you engage more mindfully with the things that tempt you (Milyavskaya, Saunders, & Inzlicht, 2020, Self-control in daily life: Prevalence and effectiveness of diverse self-control strategies).

Finally, you can postpone. Promise yourself that you will indulge later and then do it. If you make a promise to yourself and then break it, this strategy loses effectiveness (Milyavskaya, Saunders, & Inzlicht, 2020, Self-control in daily life: Prevalence and effectiveness of diverse self-control strategies).

Research suggests that either strategy can be effective in the right situation, and it's a good idea to have them in your toolbox. They all help you build effective self-control by influencing the related brain areas in different ways.

Emotional regulation

The second executive skill is emotional regulation. This can be defined as any strategy or behavior that the person uses to alter their emotional state now or in the future, considering aspects like emotional intensity and expression (Charles, 2011, Emotion Regulation).

This skill is very important and has a wide-reaching impact on everything from our well-being to our professional goals to our relationships. Learning to control our emotions involves balancing strategies that account for our needs (like emotional expression) and contextual demands (e.g., being professional). Our emotions play a huge role in the brain with structures like the limbic system and the amygdala closely tied to our feelings and how we manage them (Wilms, Lahnwer, & Kastenmuller, 2020 Emotion Regulation in Everyday Life: The Role of Goals and Situational Factors).

Technique #9 separating emotions from thoughts

One of the best and most accessible paths to emotion regulation is cognitive-behavioral therapy. Rather than addressing the emotions directly, this approach, with its many practical techniques, targets the way we think, leading to more or less intense emotions. Cognitive-behavioral therapy can help us change the brain, and it can directly affect our frontal lobe and prefrontal cortex (Chala & Ayache, 2018, Disentangling the Neural Basis of Cognitive Behavioral Therapy in Psychiatric Disorders: A Focus on Depression).

We often view emotions as something that happens beyond our control. While they can appear as reactions to what is happening around us, we can also control our emotions, especially how we express them. Eventually, through consistent work, we can even reduce the intensity of our emotions often and be able to avoid impulsive reactions that might hurt our relationships and well-being. Emotions have an important role in our day-to-day life, but regulating them is another skill with a strong neural basis.

- Reappraisal

Reappraisal involves shifting the meaning of a situation. This technique is proven to reduce activation in the amygdala. It involves trying to find alternative ways of considering a situation and interpreting it in a less negative way (Moyal, Henik, & Anholt, 2014, Cognitive strategies to regulate emotions—current evidence and future directions).

For example, you might experience a lot of anxiety when running late for an appointment. You can think about this situation in many ways that will evoke less anxiety. Rather than worrying about what people will think and how you blew it, you might consider that it could be a good way to showcase your diplomatic skills. It could be that the appointment is not that important or that you are sure to explain yourself well. You might just let it decide that it has happened so that you may focus on the future.

- Labeling

Labeling is another strategy that can help reduce the activation of the amygdala. It involves verbally naming the emotion you are feeling and why you are feeling it. Even if you know what you are feeling, it helps to express and identify it explicitly (Moyal, Henik, & Anholt, 2014, Cognitive strategies to regulate emotions—current evidence and future directions).

- Distinguishing between emotions and reality

Emotional reasoning is an irrational thinking pattern when equating our thoughts with reality. For example, you might feel angry, and through emotional reasoning, it means you were hurt and offended. Or you might think that if you are anxious, then the situation is truly dangerous. But in reality, it's useful to separate feelings from events, as our emotions are not always objective (Alkozei, Cooper, & Creswell, 2014, Emotional reasoning and anxiety sensitivity: Associations with social anxiety disorder in childhood).

Learning to accept that our emotions are subjective and not always a good reflection of reality can help us react less impulsively. First, we look for objective evidence. Is there something here that merits the reaction you are having? Are there other factors that might be influencing the way you are reacting? Distinguish between objective and subjective to reduce the impact of your emotions and regulate them better.

- Distinguishing between ideas and reality

Considering the above, we often interpret things in a certain way. Another common irrational thinking pattern is catastrophizing, which makes us assume that the worst-case scenario will happen. But it hasn't happened yet, and it's not likely to happen. The same things can happen with events from the past that cause us regret or situations we imagine are happening (e.g., I think my partner might be cheating on me and react as if it was happening) (Lazaridou et al., 2018, Effects of Cognitive-Behavioral Therapy (CBT) on brain connectivity supporting catastrophizing in fibromyalgia).

Ask yourself whether there is evidence that goes against your assumption that, say, things will turn out in the worst way possible. Is there another possibility or possibilities? What is the best case scenario? What other things might happen? Don't accept your thoughts as facts either: look for evidence against your assumptions.

This helps you reduce your emotional intensity and also trains your brain to think of situations in a more nuanced way.

These techniques help us improve emotion regulation and strengthen this aspect of our executive functioning. Even though they do not target emotions directly, their effects are very strong and have a positive long-term influence on our brains.

Working memory

Working memory is the third executive skill to discuss. It involves the ability to retain the information we need to solve a problem or deal with our situation in our minds. It contains elements from our memory and senses that we manipulate to reach a particular outcome (Cowan, 2014, Working Memory Underpins Cognitive Development, Learning, and Education).

For example, imagine that you are preparing a cake. You need to remember the information from the recipe: which ingredients you need, what amounts you must use, and what order to add them in. In addition, you might need to remember to grab the whole milk, not the almond milk, because of the taste, and pick up the salt from the pantry. All these elements are in your working memory as you work through the recipe. The more elements there are, the harder they are to remember at once, and something might slip your mind. If you have the recipe book open in front of you, you will probably not keep the whole recipe in your working memory, just the current step, and then go back to check it. Writing things down is a good way of easing the load on your working memory that can only keep a few items at a time, and then they are moved to long-term memory or are gone forever.

Working memory is hugely important for our brain. It promotes the creation of long-term memory and can also determine our performance in a variety of tasks. Lower working memory capacity can lead to worse outcomes, and it has also been linked to lower IQ measures (Cowan, 2014, Working Memory Underpins Cognitive Development, Learning, and Education).

Technique #10 Extend your working memory

Your working memory likely can operate better in an environment that is well-suited for it. Keep irrelevant information away from your mind while working and focus your attention on one thing at a time. It will also help you avoid cluttering your mental workspace too much besides the memory benefits it has. You can also use aids to help you, like post-its and a notebook or an app to keep your notes there rather than try to cram them all into your working memory space (Brogaard, 2020, Can You Improve Your Working Memory?).

However, some researchers suggest there is also a way of improving your working memory. Here, we will be recommending specific types of cognitive training.

- N-back tasks

An N-back task is a cognitive task that requires you to remember whether an image being presented appeared in the same position as the one presented before or two steps ago. You can find games that use the N-back task to create a stimulating experience for your brain and are available for free. For best results, you are encouraged to play it every day for a few weeks (Jaeggi, 2008, Dual N-back).

- Memory games

Other memory-based games can also help you train your working memory because they also require you to use this skill. You can find many games online and in apps, and it's better to start with easier tasks and build up to more challenging options. You can also create memory games for yourself, by asking yourself questions about things you have just seen, for example, or trying to repeat what you just heard.

These three skills are sure to leave a big impact on your brain and behavior, as they underlie success in many different areas of our lives. Executive functions are central to our overall performance because these are broad and underlying skills with a neural basis. If they are failing, we are likely to see a lot of negative outcomes. Even if your brain has trouble with these functions, it is possible to train specific areas to perform better, focus better, and accomplish improved results.

Takeaways

- There are countless scientifically proven techniques and methods for getting the most out of our brains.
- Technique 1 works with your innate circadian, ultradian and infradian rhythms and plans activities according to when your body is best primed to handle them. Find your unique body clock rhythms (chronotype) by observing your ebb and flow of energy, and then schedule tasks accordingly.
- Our brains prefer easy and fun things, and this preference for instant gratification can lead to procrastination. We can get

around this by deliberately making tasks appear more interesting and fun, such as by breaking them into chunks, using extrinsic or intrinsic rewards, or gamifying the process.
- The brain can prefer repetition and habit. Get out of autopilot by using novelty to get out of the default node network. Learn something new, do games and puzzles and attempt things in a novel way.
- Executive skills are those that allow us to exert fine control over our behavior. We can develop our self-control by using mediation to bring us to the moment despite distraction and a wandering mind. Resisting temptation becomes easier with practice, and strengthens our executive function.
- We can improve our emotional regulation by having CBT or cognitive behavioral therapy. We can reappraise situations and our emotional responses, distinguishing between perception and reality, and empowering proactive choice.
- Finally, we can boost our brain's recall limitations by practicing N-back tasks and other memory games that strengthen our working memory.

Chapter 4. How The Brain Learns

Learning is one of the foundational cognitive processes we have and one which distinguishes us as humans. Some animals are born with instincts, a kind of preinstalled series of behavioral patterns that tell birds to build their nests or spiders to make their webs or birds to fly south when it gets cold (Blumberg, 2016). Animals need not learn to do many things that are essential for their survival. But humans do. Even such basic things for our daily life as language must be learned, even if they do have some innate basis.

We start learning from the moment we are born, and our brain is naturally wired for it. Kids absorb information like sponges, ready to learn everything about the world, but we are ready and able to learn even as adults. This process underlies most things we do. But if we are naturally wired for learning, why do we struggle with it so much?

Once again, the answer to that is related to a lack of understanding of how learning works. When we learn to walk and talk, we do it in a way that comes naturally to our brains, no problem, but from the time we enter school, we are often taught other, less effective ways of studying. We often lose our natural motivation to learn, especially if we have bad experiences, or associate the process with tediousness and boredom. We start trying to learn by rote memorization. All these things can hurt our ability to learn in the future (Yair, 2000, Reforming Motivation: how the structure of
instruction affects students' learning experiences).

But we can make up for this by adopting better strategies for learning, specifically those that respect the brain's natural learning abilities – which are considerable! Specific negative experiences in school and beyond with learning can leave a person feeling incapable or not wired for it. While some struggle more with academic learning, specifically, it is untrue that there are people who cannot learn. Our brains are made for learning just as much as they are made for survival.

Even as adults, neuroplasticity shows we can learn whatever we want. If we can't, it's usually because we first need to develop the right skills for learning effectively or because we are missing more basic information. Here, we will focus on the evidence-based techniques that will help your brain rebuild its natural love and learning skills.

Weaving a strong neural network

We know that our brain works through association, by building neural networks. Each neuron can have hundreds and thousands of connections. The things with more and stronger associations with other aspects of our life are those that are best embedded in our networks. We are unlikely to forget our own name, for example, because it is closely tied to our personal history and identity and hundreds of experiences. The neuron responsible for our name probably has thousands of connections across the brain.

But the less embedded something is, the less likely we are to remember (Owens & Tanner, 2017, Teaching as Brain Changing: Exploring Connections between Neuroscience and Innovative Teaching). Something that is irrelevant and disconnected from our experiences and other neural networks is unlikely to stay in our minds for a long time. If you were told to remember a random number, you would struggle more with it than with a phone number for a dear friend, because this number becomes attached to a neural network.

Technique #11 Building strong connections

To enhance our learning, we need to place the new information in a context and tie it to things we already know and our experiences. Context helps the existing connections that can link to this new bit in our neural networks (Owens & Tanner, 2017, Teaching as Brain Changing: Exploring Connections between Neuroscience and Innovative Teaching).

How it connects to the brain: Learning is the process that occurs in the brain through a series of created new connections between neurons. There is a physiological basis to what we know or fail to recall. We will examine how allow us to form stronger connections that are likely to last, which translates into better and enduring learning.

If you are learning a new piece of information, consider how it connects to your life or to real life. Can you find examples in your memory that can be linked to that new bit of information? Can you link it to the media you consume or your personal history? Is there any other knowledge you can tie to this new bit of information?

Consider that you are learning the history of a country, and it's new to you. You might remember things better if you connect them to other historical facts and dates that you already know. What was going in the rest of the world during this time? Do the historical events occur to remind you of stories or facts you know? What is your personal feeling about the events, and how do they relate to your own life?

The more connections you make, the better you will remember. Personal and emotional connections to your own experience and history are even more likely to endure. Also, consider making connections that draw on as many of your five senses as possible, to give new information more dimension. You are more likely to recall a memory if you have paid attention to the sights, smells, and sounds accompanying that moment, rather than just a few abstract details.

Connections can also help us improve recall. If you need to remember something better, what can you do? Use context cues to jog your brain. Think of these retrieval cues almost as "handles" or tags that help you find and pull up stored information.

When we consolidate our learning inside our memory, we do not place the new item into a separate box. Rather, it is connected to other data and information, not just other knowledge, but also context clues. If thing A and thing B occur together, we are likely to link them in our minds. If we wanted to remember A; we could think of B, and our brains would naturally go in that direction (Osth, 2019, Giving your memories physical or emotional context may help you remember them better).

Try memorizing and learning in a similar context to make your learning more effective for a particular context. Scents, music, flavors, and other cues can help our brain remember what was going on and produce the information we want. When we are happy, it's easier to remember happy memories and things we learned while we felt happy; and the same thing happens with the other emotions. It's far easier to recall something with a powerful emotional impact on us than something that bored us. This is why mnemonics used to improve studying are so much better when they're rude, funny or outrageous – they stand out in memory!

To bring back a particular type of information or experience, place yourself in a context that can bring similar ideas to mind. Chewing a specific gum flavor while studying and during the exam, for example, can help you recall the items you learned through association. Or perhaps you study different chapters in different parts of your house. During the exam you can recall the exact day you studied a particular chapter, and you can remember details of that room – which help you recall details of the chapter.

Additional strategies to build stronger connections involve using different aids to create visual images, audio associations, and more. If you are struggling to learn something just from reading, add charts and images (or visualize what you learn as vividly as you can), podcasts and video, talk about it, and explain it to others so you can hear it in your own voice. This will strengthen the connection network and might make it easier for you to recall the information (Kalludi, Punja, Rao, & Dhar, 2015, Is Video Podcast Supplementation as a Learning Aid Beneficial to Dental Students?; Pateşan, Balagiu, & Alibec, 2018, Visual Aids in Language Education).

Add more connections for each new piece of information and connect it as much as you can to what you already know. Remember the context and associated cues. Use different ways of learning, not because of learning styles, but because they will add more connections to your network and cement the new information.

Two thinking modes

When we learn, our brain usually alternates between two modes of thinking. We have the focused mode and the diffuse mode. The focused mode is defined as the state when we focus on our activity. For example, when reading, writing, or doing calculations, our brain is likely in focused mode. Otherwise, we might have to re-read or won't be making much progress on these tasks (Oakley, 2021, A Mind for Numbers).

The diffuse mode involves allowing the mind to wander. We are not disconnected from the world, but we are not thinking of anything. Our thoughts go here and there, darting from one idea to the next. Some activities make it easy for our minds to wander, for example, doing the dishes or listening to music or doodling (Oakley, 2021, A Mind for Numbers). We can't stay focused all the time, nor can we always be distracted. The two modes are a little like a laser versus a dull, broad spotlight.

Our brain will normally alternate between the two modes of thinking. You have surely experienced it yourself. If you are trying to learn from a text, after a while, you might find your mind drifting because it cannot sustain attention for so long. But eventually, you can focus back on what you were reading. This is normal, and it can promote our learning.

Technique #12 Planning for the switches

When learning, we need to alternate between these two modes and plan to have time to engage in both. Here we can also remember our ultradian rhythms: our energy levels ebb and flow, and so does our attention. That's not a problem! During a 90-minutes learning session, we might focus and then lose focus, but both states promote our learning. To allow the information to set in our brain, we should spend a period working intently and giving our full attention to the stimuli and then do something else while it settles. Take a walk or a shower, doodle or listen to music. This is not being lazy but promoting learning in a new way (Oakley, 2021, A Mind for Numbers).

For new knowledge, we might need to let the information simmer around our brain with the diffuse mode. Otherwise, we can be left with a superficial understanding of the topic. Mind wandering allows our brain to process the information and connect it to other associations within our brain (Oakley, 2021, A Mind for Numbers). Sleep is especially useful in this way, since it allows your brain to consolidate everything it learnt and refresh itself – try drilling through something just before bed and then again when you wake up in the morning. With no effort, you'll notice that it's easier after a night's sleep.

The need for regular pauses and breaks is one reason why cramming doesn't work. When we cram, we do the focused mode throughout the session, but we don't allow the information to settle and be processed in the diffuse mode. It's like attempting to tense a muscle continuously, without a break. In other words, it doesn't work, and you only end up exhausting yourself – or getting an injury!

How it connects to the brain: We can't always voluntarily pay full attention. Our brain needs to go between different modes of processing information, and we can't ignore this aspect of our neural functioning permanently.

You can learn better by alternating between focused and diffuse mode throughout a study session. Don't be afraid to take breaks - remember that your body also needs them, and so does your brain. It will reinforce, not hurt, your learning. Just focus on the topic first for a significant period, like half an hour, an hour, or an hour and a half.

Just like you plan your average day using ultradian rhythms, plan to alternate between focused and diffuse-promoting activities. You can take a couple of hours to read, watch videos, take notes, solve the problem actively, answer questions, and then spend some time outdoors or just away from the desk. Stretch and get into your body and out of your mind. Some good ideas for the diffuse mode involve light chores, exercise, walking, being in nature, doodling or drawing, free writing, and more.

Less information is more

Can you memorize a 250-word list of random concepts? Possibly, but it will likely be difficult. But if you have to learn a poem by heart, it will probably be much easier for you to learn 250 words by heart and in order.

Why? Because of how these two types of stimuli present their information. One offers a non-organized list. The other tidily puts the information together so it is easy to process and remember. The information is organized in a way digestible for our brains and much more likely to be placed in a neural network without issue.

This process is called chunking, and it's a brilliant way to get your brain to remember more than it naturally can. Chunking involves organizing information in easily digestible "chunks" that promote learning. The quantity of information doesn't change, and neither does the quality. The only thing that changes is how it is organized and presented (Lah, Saat, & Hassan, 2014, The Malaysian Online Journal of Educational Science Cognitive Strategy in

Learning Chemistry: How Chunking and Learning Get Together).

There are different ways to chunk. We can group smaller units into a bigger chunk, for example, putting together an acronym to remember a list of concepts. We can split a big chunk of information into smaller, more manageable units, like dividing a book into chapters and the chapters into sections and so on. We might also group things depending on how they relate to each other (e.g., first and second, more important and less important, general and specific, etc.) or how similar they are (Lah, Saat, & Hassan, 2014, The Malaysian Online Journal of Educational Science Cognitive Strategy in Learning Chemistry: How Chunking and Learning Get Together).

Technique #13 How to make chunks

We can learn more effectively if we present the information in ways that are easy to process. It's hard to learn the contents of a whole book and easier to go topic by topic. It's hard to learn a dozen random words and easier to learn a phrase that brings these words together. Here are a few ways you can chunk information for easier consumption.

- Tell a story

Our brains can't get enough of stories. We can remember a well-told anecdote years after first hearing it and remember all the complex relationships of our favorite TV show characters, even if it's been going on for 100 episodes. A good story helps us remember. You can integrate the information you need to learn in a story that reflects the information's sequence. If you are learning something that has a narrative, like a historical event, or which requires understanding of cause and effect relationships, take advantage of that and integrate other information, like dates, into the story (Kulfosky, Wang, & Ceci, 2008, Do better stories make better memories? Narrative quality and memory accuracy in preschool children).

- Do a mind-map

A mind-map is a way of organizing information visually. On a sheet of paper or your drawing/mind-mapping app of choice, you can create a representation of how different ideas and concepts fit together. Summarize the information and use the image to represent how it all comes together, for example, if something is split into various categories or if two things belong on the same level. This will help you structure the information and discover the connections between separate ideas, much like our brain does it (Kalyanasundaram et al., 2017, Effectiveness of Mind Mapping Technique in Information Retrieval Among Medical College Students in Puducherry-A Pilot Study).

- Find your own way to create meaningful chunks of information

A story is one way to give information meaning, and a drawing is another. Find other solutions to construct chunks of information that make sense to you. You can tie separate into a phrase or an acronym. For example, FANBOYS is a well-known acronym that stands for, And, Nor, But, Or, Yet, and So that need to be separated by a comma when used to separate two independent clauses. FANBOYS is easier to remember.

Some people think better by drawing or doodling what they are trying to learn or creating bizarre visual images. Techniques like the memory palace involve memorizing different forms of information by placing visual images in a mental representation of a place they know well (Qureshi et al., 2014, The method of loci as a mnemonic device to facilitate learning in endocrinology leads to improvement in student performance as measured by assessments). This creates a meaningful sequence that is easy to follow and recall.

Don't try to swallow information as it is given to you. If it is unstructured, confusing, or something that you do not understand, you won't memorize it, and you won't learn it, though you might hold on to some ideas for a while. For deep learning, work with the information, so your brain is ready and willing to learn it.

Pavlov and his dogs

You might have heard of Ivan Pavlov and his dogs. Famously, this researcher taught them how to react to the sound of a bell by salivating. This reflects the same pattern: our brain learns through association. Pavlov was experimenting with his dogs and studying their digestion. Inadvertently, he created a strong association between the sound of a bell that always sounded when the food was about to come. He observed that the dogs were now reacting not to the food, but the bell, because the presentation of the two items together helped the dogs create a strong association between the two (Tully, 2003, Pavlov's dogs). The dogs learned this simple thing: if there is the sound of a bell, food is about to be presented.

While our brains are more complex than those of a dog, our learning operates in the same way. We might also develop associations with sounds, smells, experiences, and more. If your alarm always rings at 7 am, for example, you might still wake up at that hour even if it doesn't ring. There is an association between 7 am and you waking up. If you are not fond of school, the sound of a school bell might still evoke feelings of dread, even if your pupil days are far behind you.

Like habits, these associations are automatic and unconscious.

We have discussed this previously, but you can promote your learning through these little sensory associations.

Technique #14 Plant cues for your future self

You can improve your recall of past information and events by recreating the context in which you learned or experienced them. If you hear the song you associate with an ex-partner, it's easy to think of them and your relationship and go down memory lane. But don't be at the mercy of this process – you can deliberately pre-plant these cues to support your learning. Your brain will do the work for you here, and these associations can help you remember things when it becomes most important.

Wouldn't it be great if you could stimulate a precise memory using particular sensations? Theoretically, you can. If you are preparing for an exam, see whether you can study in the same room where it will take place. The context will help you remember the information more effectively. If you can replicate other elements, like a scent you are wearing or a taste you have in your mouth, it can also help. However, you should not use scents or flavors or other stimuli you experience every day, which will naturally weaken the association.

How it connects to the brain: Our brain's organized through neural networks. Activating one node in this network can make others more active. When we consciously integrate specific details or concepts into the network, it is like creating a neural path to the desired information we can retrace later.

You can use this strategy to create easy ways to pull yourself into a better mood, for example, by playing a song you enjoy only when you feel happy. Hearing that song later can nudge you towards a better emotional state, as long as you use it sparingly.

This is a smaller strategy that can help you prepare in advance. It's easy to use and relatively quick to implement.

Make learning more fun

We have talked a little about the extrinsic and intrinsic motivation for reducing your procrastination. You can apply the same strategies here, and gamification to make learning more fun. Here, you might find these strategies work just as well, especially those related to intrinsic motivation and rewards. But are there other ways to make learning more fun besides the ones we have discussed?

Technique #14 Creative learning approaches

Many people have had bad experiences in schools. They found them stifling or boring. But that should not be the attitude we have towards learning now. We have the power to make it more fun - and fun is likely to motivate our brain more thanks to the anticipation of the experience. When we associate learning with fulfilling and fun experiences, it becomes easier to motivate ourselves to learn something new.

How it connects to the brain: Creativity is a highly complex neural process. However, it appears to be one that our brains enjoy a lot and is tied to the dopaminergic system (Khalil, Godde, & Karim, 2019, The Link Between Creativity, Cognition, and Creative Drives Underlying Neural Mechanisms).

- Get creative

Creativity is difficult to describe, but it stimulates our brain and is motivational. We like being creative and finding new ways of expressing ourselves, and the more creative we are, the more creative we can be. So consider how you can be creative about your learning. How will you take notes? What will help you practice the skills? Make it a challenge for yourself to do something unexpected and look for non-standard ways of engaging with a topic (Elisondo, Ronoldo, & Dinaudo, 2013, The Unexpected and Education: Curriculums for Creativity). A benefit of this is that you are far more likely to remember and make good use of your own techniques than those you have merely adopted from other people.

As an adult learner, you have all the freedom you want to pursue your own projects and learning objectives. In other contexts, you might be a little more limited, but you still have the choice of bringing creativity whenever you can. By engaging in this way with the material or the skills, you are making it more likely that the process will be enjoyable for you. For example, many people love artistically taking notes, accompanying them with colors and stickers. Or they study in interesting or different locations each time. They make the process creative and more enjoyable, so they have more motivation to engage with the material in the way they like.

- Look for materials you are likely to enjoy

When learning something new, look for supporting materials and texts. Don't be afraid of looking for materials you want to read, watch, or listen to, even if they are unorthodox. You're in charge! There are plenty of videos and podcasts that engage with the topic in a fun way and might bring you an unexpected perspective on the situation. Likewise, you may be exposed to a teacher or speaker more on your wavelength and who stirs your passion for the topic. This doesn't mean you have to enjoy all the materials you are working with, but finding those you would explore and engage with on your own is a good way of supporting your learning experience (Hernik & Jaworska, 2018, The Effect of Enjoyment on Learning).

- Find stories that involve what you are learning

Stories are a good way of organizing information to learn. But they can support your experience and help you understand the material better. Storytelling is an effective strategy that can be applied with adult learners because it motivates, generates curiosity, and often gives us a broader perspective on the topic – remember that your brain loves connections, and it loves meaningful narratives (Enzo & Gray, 2012, The Effectiveness of Storytelling on Adult Learning). You might not influence the strategies of your instructor, if you are learning formally, but you can look for stories that connect to what you are studying. Even if the only story you can generate is to argue with your instructor, at least you are engaging authentically with the material!

There are many ways to do this. You can choose a less direct approach. Science fiction might talk about science, for example. You can look for real-life examples and stories that are much more memorable than just the facts.

Of course, stories and especially fiction, are not always accurate. But this can present a challenge of its own. How does it get things wrong? Why does it get things wrong? How would you fix it? Stories encourage us creatively and stimulate our imagination, and our brain is much more likely to remember a tale than a statistic.

Deep processing

The more we engage with a subject, the better we learn it. It's not enough to just read it and be done with it - we might need to go deeper and allow our brains more interaction with the material. This is called deep processing.

How do you ensure that you are learning in-depth and not superficially? First, do the things proven to help your brain remember and avoid the strategies proven ineffective.

Second, we have discussed how it's good for you to engage with different materials, from texts to videos, on what you are learning. Besides more associations and neural connections, this also helps us promote deep processing, as we continuously engage with a subject and reinforce what we know as we also make progress. What other strategies are there?

Technique #15 Effective study methods

First, let's mention the techniques that do not work for studying and don't lead to deep processing. Re-reading is not a good strategy. It makes us think we know something when we might not know it. Re-read to understand better but not to study better. The same applies to highlighting and underlining. It can help you find the information later but does not affect retention or recall (Oakley, 2021, A Mind for Numbers).

Then, what does work? The first strategy that is very helpful is testing yourself. Close the text or put away your notes and try to answer a few questions or solve problems. This active form of engagement guarantees you will remember things much better later on (Oakley, 2021, A Mind for Numbers).

How does this connect with the brain: Effective study strategies help reinforce our neural networks and build powerful connections between neurons that can endure even if time goes on.

Try to explain to or teach someone else what you have just learned. Animated and interested students are best. However, you can do with your reflection in the mirror, a pet, or any other person. This technique is great at revealing what you understand and don't understand and promotes better learning. It helps to explain it as simply as you can rather than reproduce the information from memory. Use your own words and style (Oakley, 2021, A Mind for Numbers).

Space your study sessions. Cramming is another ineffective approach, whether it is for a test or any other purpose. Our brains need time to strengthen the neural associations between concepts and ideas, which only happens with various repetitions over several days. To remember things for longer, you should space your repetition over a longer while (Oakley, 2021, A Mind for Numbers).

Engaging with learning on a deep level also means being more active. Try creating your own ideas, projects, or applications. Even if they stay as concepts, being proactive forces your brain to take the matter seriously and make it more memorable overall.

Learning is a basic process for our brains, but this doesn't mean we can't make it more effective. By applying the right strategies and knowing how our brain operates, we can boost our results and teach ourselves whatever we want. It just takes time and repeated effort.

Takeaways

- We can improve our capacity to learn and memorize by working with our brain's innate abilities. Learning is possible for *everyone* – we just need to use the right strategies.
- Help your brain to have a better recall by weaving a strong neural network that

makes as many neural connections between ideas as possible. Connect new pieces of information to as many other pieces of information as you can to cement it in your memory.
- There are two thinking modes – diffuse and focused. We naturally switch between these as our brain alternates effort and rest. Plan for and support these switched by scheduling breaks according to your own biological rhythms.
- The brain can only remember so much information, but it can effectively remember more if you chunk that information. You can chunk by finding narratives, making mind maps or looking for meaningful connections and associations to organize data into simpler units.
- Pavlov famously trained his dogs using classical conditioning. We can do the same when we deliberately plant cues for ourselves and build associations between stimuli and desired behaviors.
- Bad associations from early schooling can undermine our learning. We can undo these by thinking creatively and finding novel ways to bring fun to our own

processes, whether we study formally or on our own.
- Finally, deep processing is about the rich understanding we have of a topic rather than a superficial grasp. We need to learn to read for deep comprehension and *understanding*, which we can test by explaining concepts to others. We are far more likely to retain content if we process content deeply.

Chapter 5. How The Brain Memorizes

Memory, of course, is heavily related to learning. People are seldom said to have learnt something if they can't really remember any of it! This is why so many techniques and methods around learning focus on recall. As with other aspects of our cognition, however, we can drastically improve our memory if we take the time to understand its optimal function, and how we can support this for better learning.

If memory is a storage system that exists within specific neural pathways, then learning is about changing neural pathways to adapt one's behavior and thinking to the emergence of new information. They depend on each other because the goal of learning is to assimilate new knowledge into memory, and memory is useless without the ability to learn more. Many memory techniques exist, but they all truly function on the contents of this chapter.

Memorization is how we store and retrieve information for use (essentially the process of learning), and there are three steps to creating a memory. An error in any of these steps will result in knowledge that is not effectively converted to memory—a weak memory or the feeling of "I can't remember his name, but he was wearing purple..."

1. Encoding
2. Storage
3. Retrieval

Encoding is the step of processing information through your senses. We do this constantly, and you are doing it right now. We encode information both consciously and subconsciously through all of our senses. If you are reading a book, you are using your eyes to encode information, but how much attention and focus are you actually giving it? The more attention and focus you devote to an activity, the more conscious your encoding becomes—otherwise, it can be said that you subconsciously encode information, like listening to music at a café or seeing traffic pass you by at a red traffic light.

Many people mistakenly think they have a "bad memory" when it may be more accurate to say that it's a question of attention. Such a person might forget the name of someone they just met, not because they have a faulty memory, but because they simply weren't paying much attention when they were introduced—but they do remember in great detail the adorable dog on a lead walking past at just that moment.

How much focus and attention you devote also determines how strong the memory is and, consequently, whether that memory only makes it to your short-term memory or if it passes through the gate to your long-term memory. If you are reading a book while watching television, your encoding is probably not too deep or strong. Similarly, you are more likely to remember something that has strong emotional significance for you when compared with something that doesn't really concern you beyond the intellectual level.

Storage is the next step after you've experienced information with your senses and encoded it. What happens to the information once it passes through your eyes or ears? There are three choices for where this information can go, and they determine whether it's a memory that you will consciously know exists. There are essentially three memory systems: sensory memory, short-term memory, and long-term memory.

The last step of the memory process is **retrieval**, which is when we actually use our memories and can be said to have learned something. You might be able to recall it from nothing, or you might need a cue to bring the memory up. Other memories might only be memorized in a sequence or as part of a whole, like reciting the ABCs and then realizing you need to sing to remember how it goes. Usually, however much attention you devoted to the storage and encoding phases of memory determines just how easy it is to retrieve those memories. Most of the learning process isn't necessarily focused on retrieval—it's concentrated on the storage aspect and what you can do to force information from sensory and short-term areas into long-term ones.

Think about when you cram for a test. You want information you experience to be in your brain for perhaps 24 hours, which means it has to exist beyond short-term memory and certainly beyond sensory memory. You might not care if you remember this information about the French Revolution at the end of the year, so you will reach a level of attention and focus that will push the information into the hazy area between short- and long-term memory. In reality, what's happening is that you will rehearse the information enough to make a very faint imprint on your long-term memory. But after that, the impression fades pretty quickly.

Accelerating your learning, in a sense, is the same as improving your memory capacity and how absorbent your memory is—the more sponge-like, the better. It's also about giving you conscious control over the steps of the process that normally run automatically. If you know how and why your memory works, you can squeeze the most out of it!

Forgetting

However, learning is both the process of improving memory while also getting better at *not forgetting*. Why do we forget? Why can't we remember this fact? How did we ever let something slip from our brains?

As you have read, forgetting is usually a failure or shortcoming in the storage process—the information you want only makes it to short-term memory, not long-term. The problem isn't that you can't find the information in your brain; it's that the information wasn't embedded strongly enough to begin with. This may have happened partly because you never cemented the memory by recalling it again and again; i.e., you didn't strengthen those tentative neural connections and your brain, seeing that they weren't really needed, let them go.

Sometimes it's easier to think about forgetting as a failure in learning. There are generally three different ways you retrieve or access your memories:

1. Recall

2. Recognition
3. Relearning

Recall is when you remember a memory without external cues. It's when you can recite something on command in a vacuum—for example, looking at a blank piece of paper and then writing down the capitals of all of the countries of the world. When you can recall something, you have the strongest memory of it. You have either rehearsed it enough or attached enough significance to it so that it is an incredibly strong memory within your long-term memory. You go into your brain's storage, find exactly what you're looking for, and reproduce it in full.

Of course, because recall represents the strongest level of memory, it's also typically the toughest to achieve. It would generally require hours of rehearsal or study to get anywhere close to this level. However, once we acquire information this way, the benefit is that it's a lot harder to un-learn or forget. When we study, we want information to enter this realm, but we will usually settle for the next type of memory retrieval.

Recognition is when you can conjure up your memory in the presence of an external cue. It's when you might not be able to remember something by pure recall, but if you get a small clue or reminder, you will remember it. For example, you might not be able to recall all of the capitals of the world, but if you got a clue such as the first letter of the capital or something that rhymes with it, it would be fairly easy to state it. This "jogs your memory" enough that you can carry on once you get started.

When we cram information, recognition is typically what we end up with. This is also how mnemonics and similar memory devices work. We know we aren't able to definitively store and recall so many pieces of information without a massive amount of rehearsal, so we work on chunking information into easily recognizable cues. With the right cue, we are pointed in the right direction and can gradually access memories stored a little less concretely.

Relearning is undoubtedly the weakest form of recall. It occurs when you are relearning or reviewing information and it takes you less effort each subsequent time. For example, if you read a list of country capitals on Monday and it takes you 30 minutes, it should take you 15 minutes the next day, and so on. Unfortunately, this is where we mostly lie on a daily basis. We might be familiar with a concept, but we haven't committed enough of it to memory to avoid essentially relearning it when we look at it again.

This is what happens when we are new to a topic or we've forgotten most of it already. When you're in the relearning stage, you essentially haven't taken anything past the barrier of short-term memory into long-term memory. From your brain's perspective, this kind of information is simply not important, relevant or repeated enough to warrant more space in your memory.

The Forgetting Curve

Not only are we fighting weak encoding or storage in our quest for learning, we are also fighting the brain's natural tendency to forget as soon as possible.

This is encapsulated by the *forgetting curve*, a concept pioneered by psychologist Hermann Ebbinghaus. Below is a picture of the forgetting curve, courtesy of Wranx.com.

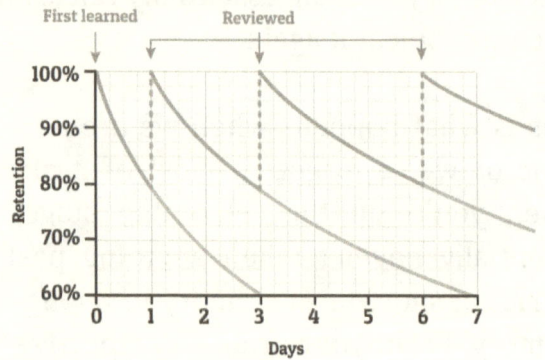

Typical Forgetting Curve for Newly Learned Information

This shows the rate of memory decay and forgetting over time if there is no attempt to move information into long-term memory. If you read something about the French Revolution on Monday, then you'll typically remember only half of it after four days and retain as little as 30% at around a week's time. If you don't review what you've learned, it's very likely you will only retain 10% of what you learned about the French Revolution.

However, if you review and rehearse it, you can see in the graph above how you will retain and memorize more over time. You will bump the retention level back up to 100%, and then the graph will start to become shallower, indicating less decay. It's as though you are teaching your brain, "This is important. I keep needing to know this, so remember it."

The goal is to make the forgetting curve shallower—to make it resemble a horizontal line as much as possible. That would indicate very little decay, and doing that requires constant review and rehearsal.

Ebbinghaus found patterns for memory loss and isolated two simple factors that affected the forgetting curve. First, the rate of decay was significantly blunted if the memory was strong and powerful and had personal significance to the person. Second, the amount of time and how old the memory was determined how quickly and severely it decayed. This suggests there is little we can do about forgetting other than to come up with tactics to assign personal significance to information and rehearse more often.

As you can see, forgetting isn't as simple as having something on the tip of your tongue or rummaging through the stores of your brain. There are very specific processes that make it a near-miracle we actually retain as much as we do. You're probably also noticing that improving your memory is as much about good encoding and attention as it is proper rehearsing and recall.

Being able to recall information is always the goal, but more realistically, we should be shooting for recognition and to learn how to expertly use cues and hints in our daily lives. I may not be able to recite the lyrics of my favorite songs, but I can sure remember them if I hear the melody. If I become expert at managing cues for myself, I can work around the unavoidable limits of my memory.

The study cycle

Another way to work with the brain and the inbuilt mechanisms of memory is to use what's called the study cycle. Rather than one technique, this approach is about using a series of different techniques in a particular order, for a particular duration, to maximize learning. In fact, the principles behind the study cycle could explain why tactics such as retrieval practice and spaced repetition work so well.

The cycle consists of five sequential steps to follow. It will help you cement new material and, as you do so, you'll build a deeper sense of confidence in yourself as you gain knowledge and build on each new development. The cycle is also great for keeping yourself organized and motivated. Often, when we sit down to simply "study," the intention is so vague that we only waste time and miss out on an opportunity to really learn well. But with a structured, flowing study cycle, we know where we stand—and we can apply the steps to any coursework we like.

The steps are preview, attend, review, study, and assess... and then the cycle is repeated.

The first step is to **preview**. Don't just dive in; rather, begin by trying to get a broad overview of what you're doing, in what context, and why. See the big picture. What this looks like will depend on you and the subject you're studying.

For example, if you're reading through an important chapter in a textbook, you might need to start with some skimming, i.e. read through the main headings and subheadings, scan any pictures and diagrams with their titles, look at any summaries at the end, data such as graphs or tables, and bolded sections or pull quotes that have been highlighted as important. This way, you prime and cue your learning.

If your studies are taking a less traditional form, you might still like to begin by going through the material quickly to get an overview. Look through a piece of music quickly and note the time signature, the tempo, the key, and get an idea of the melody. If you're going through some academic journal articles, go through the abstracts first and broadly see what the research question, methodology and conclusions were in each before reading in detail.

The next step is to **attend**, i.e. pay attention. Crucially, the preview section helps you direct *where* your attention goes (that is, onto the most important concepts), but in the second step, you need to apply that attention fully. Here, you want to be as focused and aware as possible. Don't just sit in a lecture passively, or watch a tutorial video without taking notes.

Read or watch *actively*. This means you engage with the data coming in. Make notes, ask questions (who, what, where, when, why, how), and have a "dialogue" with the material. Jot questions in book margins and find out how to answer them. Make summaries or simplified diagrams—and use as many of your senses as possible when you encode this new information. When you generate your own study aids and explain the concepts to yourself, you'll comprehend better, and retain more.

For step 3, we **review**. Just as we previewed, now we look again and see what ground we've covered, and what material has been absorbed. Just the act of revisiting what you've taken in reinforces it further. At the end of your study session, stop and take stock. Look again through your notes and summaries, and perhaps even answer some questions you had at the beginning of the session.

You are in essence skimming again, but this time, instead of seeing the big picture of what you are going to learn, you do a quick survey of what you have learnt. Drill a few new concepts, revisit the main themes, and just take a moment to let everything sink in. If you practice retrieval immediately after learning some new data, you are teaching your brain not only to file away important information, but to cement a path via which you can search for and recall that data later on.

Step 4 is to **study**. The material is there, now you need to make sure it's taking root in your brain, permanently. The key to this? Repetition. For around 30 to 50 minutes, go over concepts, definitions, problems or ideas, reinforcing your understanding. Pay attention to those parts that are most difficult for you, but remember to keep seeing each unit in relation to the whole. Here, you can draw on all the previous steps to sit with the material and encode it into your brain.

The last step is to **assess**. Here, you want to check how well the process is going. Check how much you've retained, but also ask yourself how well your study techniques are working. Try some tests or worked problems and appraise your performance and memory. Based on the outcome, adjust your approach next time.

You'll know you've properly absorbed the material when you are able to confidently teach the concepts to another person, and feel that you comprehend enough to reproduce it or score well on a test. On the other hand, you might do well with the material but wish to change the study approach, for example spending more or less time on different steps, or using a different active reading technique.

When you're done, you start again with step one!

Retrieval Practice

So how can we use this knowledge about our memories to be more effective learners? There is one major technique that applies the fickle nature of memory: *retrieval practice*.

We typically consider learning something we absorb—something that goes *into* our brains: the teacher or textbook spits facts, data, equations, and words out at us, and we just sit there and collect them. It's merely accumulation—a very *passive* act.

This kind of relationship with learning returns knowledge that we don't retain for very long because, even though we *get* it, we don't *do* much with it. For best results, we have to make learning an *active* operation.

That's where retrieval practice comes into play. Instead of putting more stuff *in* our brains, retrieval practice helps us take knowledge *out* of our brains and put it to use. That seemingly small change in thinking dramatically improves our chances of retaining and remembering what we learn. Everyone remembers flashcards from childhood days. The fronts of the cards had math equations, words, science terms, or images, and the backs had the "answer"—the solution, definition, explanation, or whatever response the student is expected to give.

The idea of flashcards sprouts from a strategy called *retrieval practice*. This approach is neither new nor very complicated: it's simply recalling information you've already learned (the back of the flashcard) when prompted by a certain image or depiction (the front).

Retrieval practice is one of the best ways to increase your memory and fact retention. But even though its core is quite simple, actually using retrieval practice isn't quite as straightforward as just passively drilling with flashcards or scanning over notes we've taken. Rather, retrieval practice is an active skill: truly struggling, thinking, and processing to finally get to the point of recalling that information without clues—much of what we've discussed already in this book that accelerates learning.

Pooja Agarwal researched pupils taking middle school social studies over the course of a year and a half ending in 2011. The study aimed to determine how regularly scheduled, uncounted quizzes—basically, retrieval practice exercises—benefitted the ability to learn and retain.

The class teacher didn't alter their study plan and simply instructed as normal. The students were given regular quizzes—

developed by the research team—on class material with the understanding that the results would *not* count against their grades.

These quizzes only included about a third of the material covered by the teacher, who also had to leave the room while the quiz was being taken. This was so the teacher had no knowledge of what subjects the quizzes covered. During class, the teacher taught and reviewed the class as usual, without knowing which parts of the instruction were being asked on the quizzes.

The results of this study were measured during end-of-unit exams and were quite dramatic. Students scored one full grade level higher on the material the quizzes covered—the one-third of what the whole class covered—than the questions *not* asked on the no-stakes quizzes. The mere act of being occasionally tested, with no pressure to get all the answers right to boost their overall grades, actually helped students learn better.

Agarwal's study also provided insight on what kind of questions helped the most. Questions that required the student to actually recall the information from scratch yielded more success than multiple-choice questions, in which the answer could be recognized from a list, or true/false questions. The active mental effort to remember the answer, with no verbal or visual prompt, improved the students' learning and retention.

Using Retrieval Practice in Our Lives

The principal benefit of retrieval practice is that it encourages an *active* exertion of effort rather than the passive seepage of external information. When we learn something once and then actually *do* something else to reinforce our learning, it has more of an effect than merely reviewing notes or re-reading passages in books.

The knowledge that we store in our memory is activated when it's called out. Retrieval practice stimulates that movement and makes it easier to learn and retain new understandings. If we pull concepts *out* of our brain, it's more effective than just continually trying to put concepts *in*. The learning comes from taking what's been added to our knowledge and bringing it out at a later time.

We mentioned flashcards at the top of this section, and how they're an offshoot of retrieval practice. But flashcards are not, in and of themselves, the strategy: you *can* use them and still not be conducting true retrieval practice.

Many students use flashcards somewhat inactively: they see the prompt, answer it in their heads, tell themselves they know it, flip over to see the answer, and then move on to the next one. Turning this into *practice*, however, would be taking a few seconds to actually recall the answer and, at best, say the answer out loud before flipping the card over. The difference seems slight and subtle, but it's important. Students will get more advantages from flashcards by actually retrieving and vocalizing the answer before moving on.

In real-world situations—where there's usually not an outside teacher, premade flashcards, or other assistance—how can we repurpose what we learn for retrieval practice? One good way is to expand flashcards to make them more "interactive."

The flashcards in our grade-school experiences, for the most part, were very one-note. You can adapt the methodology of flashcards for more complex, real-world applications or self-learning by taking a new approach to what's on the back of the cards, as suggested by writer Rachel Adragna.

When you're studying material for work or class, make flashcards with concepts on the front and definitions on the back. After completing this task, make another set of cards that give "instructions" on how to reprocess the concept for a creative or real-life situation. Here's an example:

- "Rewrite this concept in plain English."

- "Write a movie or novel plot that demonstrates this concept."

- "Use this concept to describe a real-life event."

- "Describe the *opposite* of this concept."

- "Draw a picture of this concept."

The possibilities are, as they say, limitless in how you can seek retrieval. Using these exercises extracts more information about the concept that you produce yourself. Placing them in the context of a creative narrative or expression will help you understand them when they come up in real life. Our memories are fickle, and they like to play tricks on us by design, but they can be molded to our advantage in learning more quickly.

Spaced Repetition

This method is directly aimed at dealing with beating forgetting. Spaced repetition—otherwise known as distributed practice—is just what it sounds like.

The reason it is such an important technique in improving your memory is that it battles forgetting directly and allows you to work within the bounds of your brain's capabilities. Other techniques, no less important, are about increasing encoding or storage—remember the three parts of memory are encoding, storage, and retrieval. Spaced repetition helps the last part, retrieval.

In order to commit more to memory and retain information better, space out your rehearsal and exposure to it over as long of a period as possible. In other words, you will remember something far better if you study it for one hour a day versus twenty hours in one weekend. This goes for just about everything you could possibly learn. Additional research has shown that seeing something twenty times in one day is far less effective than seeing something ten times over the course of seven days.

Spaced repetition makes more sense if you imagine your brain as a muscle. Muscles can't be exercised all the time and then put back to work with little-to-no recovery. Your brain needs time to make connections between concepts, create muscle memory, and generally become familiar with something. Sleep has been shown to be where neural connections are made, and it's not just mental. Synaptic connections are formed in your brain, and dendrites are stimulated.

If an athlete works out too hard in one session like you might be tempted to in studying, one of two things will happen. The athlete will either be too exhausted, and the latter half of the workout will be useless, or the athlete will become injured. Rest and recovery are necessary to the task of learning, and sometimes effort isn't what's required.

Here's a look at what a schedule focused on spaced repetition might look like.

Monday at 10:00 a.m. Learn initial facts about Spanish history. You accumulate five pages of notes.

Monday at 8:00 p.m. Review notes about Spanish history, but don't just review passively. Make sure to try to recall the information from your own memory. Recalling is a much better way to process information than simply rereading and reviewing. This might only take twenty minutes.

Tuesday at 10:00 a.m. Try to recall the information without looking at your notes much. After you first try to actively recall as much as possible, go back through your notes to see what you missed, and make note of what you need to pay closer attention to. This will probably take only fifteen minutes.

Tuesday at 8:00 p.m. Review notes. This will take ten minutes.

Wednesday at 4:00 p.m. Try to independently recall the information again, and only look at your notes once you are done to see what else you have missed. This will take only ten minutes. Make sure not to skip any steps.

Thursday at 6:00 p.m. Review notes. This will take ten minutes.

Friday at 10:00 a.m. Active recall session. This will take ten minutes.

Looking at this schedule, note that you are only studying an additional seventy-five minutes throughout the week, but that you've managed to go through the entire lesson a whopping six additional times. Not only that, you've likely committed most of it to memory because you are using active recall instead of passively reviewing your notes.

You're ready for a test the next Monday. Actually, you're ready for a test by Friday afternoon. Spaced repetition gives your brain time to process concepts and make its own connections and leaps because of the repetition.

Think about what happens when you have repeated exposure to a concept. For the first couple of exposures, you may not see anything new. As you get more familiar with it and stop going through the motions, you begin to examine it on a deeper level and think about the context surrounding it. You relate it to other concepts or information, and you generally make sense of it below surface level.

All of this, of course, is designed to push information from your short-term memory into your long-term memory. That's why cramming or studying at the last minute isn't an effective means of learning. Very little tends to make it into long-term memory because of the lack of repetition and deeper analysis. At that point, it becomes rote memorization instead of the concept learning we discussed earlier, which is destined to fade far more quickly.

When you set out to learn something, instead of measuring the number of hours you spend on something, try instead to measure the number of times you revisit the same information after the initial learning. Make it your goal to increase the frequency of reviewing, not necessarily the duration. Both matter, but the literature on spaced repetition or distributed practice makes clear that breathing room is necessary.

It's true that this type of optimal learning takes up more time and planning than most of us are used to. However, if you find yourself short on time, you can still use it strategically.

To cram for a test, exam, or other type of evaluation, we don't need material to make it to our long-term memory. We just need it to make it slightly past our working memory and be partially encoded into our long-term memory. We don't need to be able to recall anything the day after, so it's like we only need something to stick for a few hours.

You might not be able to do true spaced repetition if you are cramming at the last minute, but you can simulate it in a small way. Instead of studying subject X for three hours only at night, seek to study it one hour each three times a day with a few hours between each exposure.

Recall that memories need time to be encoded and stick in the brain. You are doing the best imitation of spaced repetition you can with what you have available. To get the most out of your limited studying time, study something, for example, as soon as you wake up, and then review it at noon, 4:00 p.m., and 9:00 p.m. The point is to review throughout the day and get as much repetition as possible. Remember to focus on frequency rather than duration.

During the course of your repetition, make sure to study your notes out of order to see them in different contexts and encode more effectively. Also, use active recall versus passive reading. Don't be afraid to even intersperse unrelated material to reap the benefits of interleaved practice. Make sure to focus on the underlying concepts that govern the information you are learning so you can make educated guesses about what you don't remember.

Make sure that you're reciting and rehearsing new information up to the last minute before your test. Your short-term memory can hold seven items on its best day, so you might just save yourself with a piece of information that was never going to fit into your long-term memory. It's like you're juggling. It's inevitable that you'll drop everything, but it could just so happen that you're juggling something you can use. Make use of all types of memory you can consciously employ.

Spaced repetition, as you can see, approaches learning from a different perspective—in practicing retrieval and shooting for frequency as opposed to duration to improve memory. Even in situations where you don't have as much time as you'd like, you can use spaced repetition to cram for tests and overall just get more information into your brain—again, by focusing on frequency and not duration. When you spread out your learning and memorizing over a longer period of time and revisit the same material frequently, you'll be better off.

Takeaways

- Learning relies on memory, and memory is in turn an interplay between two processes: storing and retrieving information. There are three main steps: encoding, storing and retrieval.

- How well we **encode** material (i.e. cement it into our minds) depends on the degree and intensity of attention we pay it, as well as the senses through which we encounter it, and our associated emotions.

- When we **store** memories, we do so either as transient sensory memory, short-term memory or more long-term memory.

- **Retrieval** is when we return to stored memories and pull them out again, either with a cue or helpful sequence, or without one. We can retrieve information in a few ways: recall it directly (no cues, this is obviously preferable), recognition (remembering something after a cue or prompt, and relearning, which is the least effective and lasting method.)

- Forgetting is a normal state of affairs, and occurs on a "forgetting curve." Every time we rehearse, however, we refresh this memory, and the subsequent forgetting trails off at a less steep curve. The goal is to rehearse until the curve eventually flattens, and the rate of decay slows enough for you to say, "I've permanently learnt this."

- The study cycle is a process to follow to maximize your learning process given the way memory works. The steps are: preview, attend, review, study and assess, and then begin the cycle again. In a study session, it's best to flow through each step consciously—establishing context, paying attention, actively reading and engaging, drilling the material and then taking time to assess how well the process went afterwards.

- Retrieval practice is the art of practicing what most cements memories—retrieving them. It is an active process and instills memory firmly.

- Spaced repetition is most effective for practicing retrieval and countering forgetting. Deliberate practice, too, can help you control what you're practicing, and how this can enhance your learning and knowledge over time.

Summary Guide

CHAPTER 1. THE UNIVERSE INSIDE OUR HEADS

- The brain is a truly amazing organ and it lies at the very heart of what makes us human beings. To maximize our own potential, we need to learn how our brains work, why, and what we can do to support our innate capacities for maximum wellbeing.
- The brain's structure tells us a lot about its function. It forms part of the body's overall central nervous system. There are three main parts: the brain stem, the cerebellum, and the "higher brain" or cerebral cortex, further divided into four sections. The brain is made of billions of neurons connected neurochemically across gaps called synapses.

- The gut and its microbiome are like a "second brain" and the gut and brain are intimately connected.
- The amygdala is important for emotional processing, and the hippocampus is heavily involved in memory. Key neurotransmitters include serotonin and dopamine, although there are over 100 neurotransmitters in the brain.
- Many brain disorders and mental health issues are understood to correlate with certain chemical brain states, and the brain also possesses flaws and weaknesses that make it prone to malfunctioning.
- Neuroplasticity is the brain's ability to change and adapt to reflect demands from the environment. This means that neural connections can be "rewired," and the brain can evolve, adapt, and change, not just in childhood but throughout life.
- Many things affect neuroplasticity, such as stress, physical activity, sleep, illness, diet and other lifestyle factors. If we understand how to work with our brain's innate capacity to change itself, we can use specially designed techniques to maximize on our potential.

CHAPTER 2. THE BRAIN IS NOT PERFECT, BUT WE CAN WORK WITH IT

- Improving our lives is difficult primarily because we lack the knowledge of how to do so and the right tools. But it's also intrinsically difficult because of our brain's natural weaknesses and flaws.
- We can use scientifically proven general strategies for helping us achieve our goals, given our brain's drawbacks.
- One issue is that we cannot force our way out of acquired habit by willpower alone, and we cannot use neural connections that simply aren't there. But we can build connections with every repetition until it becomes automatic. Behaviors consist of triggers, routines and rewards. We can work with this habit loop and re-engineer the habits we already have, so the desired behavior becomes easy and automatic – with time! Consistency is key.
- Brains have limited attentional capacity, and multitasking comes with a switching cost. We can tweak our environment to make the most of our attention and be

more productive: we can fine-tune our scheduling strategy, use "time-boxing" and cut down on distractions. It's easier to get into a "flow state" when we focus on one task at a time without distraction.
- Cognitive biases are distortions in our judgments and perceptions, and can undermine our ability to think clearly, especially if they're unconscious. To make more objective decisions, acknowledge that you may be susceptible to bias, seek contrary perspectives, reframe the problem and don't act in haste.
- Finally, we can use our need for identity to support good habit formation by seeking communities with shared values and deliberately attaching that identity to ourselves.

CHAPTER 3. PEAK PERFORMANCE AND EXECUTIVE FUNCTIONING

- There are countless scientifically proven techniques and methods for getting the most out of our brains.
- Technique 1 works with your innate circadian, ultradian and infradian rhythms

and plans activities according to when your body is best primed to handle them. Find your unique body clock rhythms (chronotype) by observing your ebb and flow of energy, and then schedule tasks accordingly.
- Our brains prefer easy and fun things, and this preference for instant gratification can lead to procrastination. We can get around this by deliberately making tasks appear more interesting and fun, such as by breaking them into chunks, using extrinsic or intrinsic rewards, or gamifying the process.
- The brain can prefer repetition and habit. Get out of autopilot by using novelty to get out of the default node network. Learn something new, do games and puzzles and attempt things in a novel way.
- Executive skills are those that allow us to exert fine control over our behavior. We can develop our self-control by using mediation to bring us to the moment despite distraction and a wandering mind. Resisting temptation becomes easier with practice, and strengthens our executive function.

- We can improve our emotional regulation by having CBT or cognitive behavioral therapy. We can reappraise situations and our emotional responses, distinguishing between perception and reality, and empowering proactive choice.
- Finally, we can boost our brain's recall limitations by practicing N-back tasks and other memory games that strengthen our working memory.

CHAPTER 4. HOW THE BRAIN LEARNS

- We can improve our capacity to learn and memorize by working with our brain's innate abilities. Learning is possible for *everyone* – we just need to use the right strategies.
- Help your brain to have a better recall by weaving a strong neural network that makes as many neural connections between ideas as possible. Connect new pieces of information to as many other pieces of information as you can to cement it in your memory.

- There are two thinking modes – diffuse and focused. We naturally switch between these as our brain alternates effort and rest. Plan for and support these switched by scheduling breaks according to your own biological rhythms.
- The brain can only remember so much information, but it can effectively remember more if you chunk that information. You can chunk by finding narratives, making mind maps or looking for meaningful connections and associations to organize data into simpler units.
- Pavlov famously trained his dogs using classical conditioning. We can do the same when we deliberately plant cues for ourselves and build associations between stimuli and desired behaviors.
- Bad associations from early schooling can undermine our learning. We can undo these by thinking creatively and finding novel ways to bring fun to our own processes, whether we study formally or on our own.
- Finally, deep processing is about the rich understanding we have of a topic rather than a superficial grasp. We need to learn

to read for deep comprehension and *understanding*, which we can test by explaining concepts to others. We are far more likely to retain content if we process content deeply.

CHAPTER 5. HOW THE BRAIN MEMORIZES

- Learning relies on memory, and memory is in turn an interplay between two processes: storing and retrieving information. There are three main steps: encoding, storing and retrieval.

- How well we **encode** material (i.e. cement it into our minds) depends on the degree and intensity of attention we pay it, as well as the senses through which we encounter it, and our associated emotions.

- When we **store** memories, we do so either as transient sensory memory, short-term memory or more long-term memory.

- **Retrieval** is when we return to stored memories and pull them out again, either with a cue or helpful sequence, or without one. We can retrieve information in a few ways: recall it directly (no cues, this is obviously preferable), recognition (remembering something after a cue or prompt, and relearning, which is the least effective and lasting method.)

- Forgetting is a normal state of affairs, and occurs on a "forgetting curve." Every time we rehearse, however, we refresh this memory, and the subsequent forgetting trails off at a less steep curve. The goal is to rehearse until the curve eventually flattens, and the rate of decay slows enough for you to say, "I've permanently learnt this."

- The study cycle is a process to follow to maximize your learning process given the way memory works. The steps are: preview, attend, review, study and assess, and then begin the cycle again. In a study session, it's best to flow through each step consciously—establishing context, paying attention, actively reading and engaging, drilling the material and then taking time to assess how well the process went afterwards.

- Retrieval practice is the art of practicing what most cements memories—retrieving them. It is an active process and instills memory firmly.

- Spaced repetition is most effective for practicing retrieval and countering forgetting. Deliberate practice, too, can help you control what you're practicing, and how this can enhance your learning and knowledge over time.

www.ingramcontent.com/pod-product-compliance
Lightning Source LLC
Chambersburg PA
CBHW060355080526
44583CB00012B/317